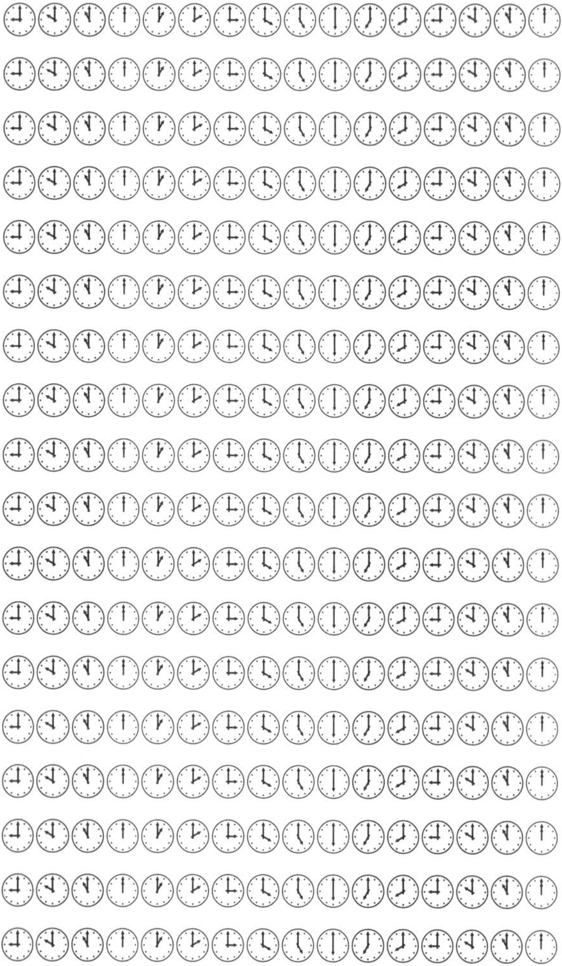

THE SERMONS

Art issues. Press
Los Angeles

SERIES EDITOR: GARY KORNBLAU

The Invisible Dragon: Four Essays on Beauty, by Dave Hickey

The World of Jeffrey Vallance: Collected Writings 1978–1994

Last Chance for Eden: Selected Art Criticism by Christopher Knight 1979–1994

Mythomania: Fantasies, Fables, and Sheer Lies in Contemporary American Popular Art by Bernard Welt

Air Guitar: Essays on Art & Democracy, by Dave Hickey

Deep Design: Nine Little Art Histories, by Libby Lumpkin

The New Now Sounds of Today! Songpoems by 21 Contemporary Artists (CD)

To order or for more information contact:

Art issues. Press
8721 Santa Monica Boulevard, #6
Los Angeles CA 90069
Telephone [323] 876-4508

Distributed Art Publishers (D.A.P.)
155 Avenue of the Americas
New York NY 10013
Telephone [800] 338-BOOK

THE SERMONS OF REVEREND
Ethan Acres

This copy has been published by Smart Art Press
in association with

Art issues. Press
Los Angeles

Art issues. Press
The Foundation for Advanced
Critical Studies, Inc.
8721 Santa Monica Boulevard, #6
Los Angeles, California 90069

FIRST EDITION

Art issues Press wishes to thank Tom Patchett and Pilar Perez at Smart Art Press for their assistance with this publication.

Library of Congress Control
Number: 2001130364
International Standard Book
Number: 0-9637264-7-1

Manufactured in the
United States of America

Contents

Call to Worship

"I AM THE ALPHA . . ."

IMAGINE a field of beautiful goldenrod, the bright yellow stalks swaying back and forth beneath a sky of the deepest blue. It is 1941, and the field lies at the outskirts of the tiny community known as Rose Hill, Mississippi. The meadow is usually quiet, dozing happily under the spell of the cicadas' lullaby. But not today. For on this hot and sticky Sunday afternoon, there is no peace, no rest. The quiet has been chased away by the sound of elated screams and laughter. Through the grass run six young boys. Their tanned legs flash in the bright sunlight as they race along, leaping into the air and occasionally falling together in a heap, only to spring back up and continue their drunken rampage. They have spent the day together, skipping church to go fishing down at Oldy Masterson's farm and to chase imaginary German soldiers through the tall oaks and pines that would one day be known as the Bienville National Forest.

Their captain, their leader, the guy who could bait a hook with his toes and would, without question, spit right in the Fuehrer's eye if he ever got the chance, was a lean, cherub-faced boy named Albert Satcher. The son of Cletus and Irma Satcher was beloved in Rose Hill, with his ebony hair, pale marblelike skin, deep blue eyes that seemed to cut right through a person, and a voice that seemed too old and deep to belong to an eleven-year-old. "The voice of an angel," Pastor Slaughter was known to remark of Albert, following the numerous occasions Irma would badger her son into reading scripture aloud to the Congregation of Sunrise Pentecostal Church.

But today, Albert was free . . . free to race and spit and smoke rabbit tobacco. Free to be just a boy. Free to run. And run he did. The others could barely keep up as Albert tore across the field, climbed over an old wooden fence, and, leaping a gully, slid to a stop in the dusty gravel of Old Pass Road. A few moments later, the rest of the brigade caught up . . . loudly cursing when they almost ran into the motionless Albert.

"Hey, Al, c'mon . . . why'd you stop?" loudly questioned Jimmy Miller.

"Maybe he heard his mama calling him?" wheezed Fatty Johnson, bent over double, trying to catch his breath.

But Albert ignored them. He stood there, one hand up over his brow, shading his eyes, as he stared up at a tall pole that stood beside the road. The other boys, having grown quiet in response to Albert's silence, all crowded around him and curiously followed his gaze. The pole was pitch black, tall and slender with a cross bar at the top. It hadn't been there a few weeks earlier, this pole, when the boys had ridden together in the back of Cletus's old Ford to get soda pops and peanuts down in Jasper. But now, here it was, stretching up into the sky like some great raven's claw, scratching away at the ceiling of the world.

"Hey look, fellas, there's another one on down the road there!" exclaimed Jimmy.

Sure enough, there was another pole, and after a little investigation, coupled with a whole lot of excited discussion, the boys realized that there appeared to be a whole slew of poles, marching along the road, probably all the way south to Jasper, as Fatty theorized, and probably, as Jimmy piped in, all the way up north, maybe even to Meridian.

"Do you guys see them wires running between 'em? What do you figure them wires are for?" mumbled Jesse Medford. To the puzzlement of all, Jesse was right; there *were* wires running from pole to pole. After several ridiculous possibilities were presented, Fatty satisfied everyone with his proposal that the wires were, in fact, telephone lines. "You know," Fatty continued, "I bet somebody could see clear to Raleigh if he stood up on top of that pole." Excited chattering erupted. Everyone agreed that somebody should climb to the top of the pole and take a look. But who would it be?

"I'll do it," said Albert. And, without waiting for any argument, Albert walked up to the pole, wrapped his skinny arms and legs around its trunk, and began to shimmy up into the sky. Slowly, he climbed. At the halfway mark, he slipped, the rough hewn skin of the pole tearing sadistically at his palms and thighs. When he finally stopped his slide, seemingly by nothing short of sheer force of will, Albert almost decided to give up this fool's errand and return to the ground, but the cheers of "ALBERT! ALBERT! ALBERT!" from below reignited his burning desire to reach his goal, and so, groaning and cursing, he continued his ascent.

At the top, Albert paused, breathing deeply, sucking long and hard at air that tasted of honeysuckle and wild juniper. Then, with all of his remaining strength, he heaved up over the crossbar, pulled up his feet and planted them squarely beside his hands. Releasing his hold, he stood straight up, balancing atop the narrow beam some forty feet in the air.

There was no noise, except the deep warble of the wind in his ears. Albert stood there, looking down at his shoes. The two cables, running across the top of the crossbar, resembled two snakes basking in the hot sun, but Albert pondered them only for a moment. He raised his head, and gasped. Before him stretched the whole wide world: a patchwork of greens and blues running away from his perch to a point where the land seemed to join the sky. Off to the left, he could see the McKinney's farm, and, turning to the right, past the fields of goldenrod and a copse of poplar trees, he spied his own house. Squinting, he just could make out his dog Beulah sleeping on the front step. Albert felt powerful. For the first time in his life, he felt bigger than the whole world. A demon of pride entered his heart. Fearlessly raising his hands above his head, he yelled into the wind, "I AM ALBERT THE GREAT!!! I AM ALBERT THE MIGHTY!!!" Looking down at his friends, undaunted by the slight tickle of vertigo's hungry tongue, he screamed "You there, little ants, look at YOU!!! You are small, but I AM TALL!!! FATTY, FATTY WHO'S YOUR DADDY? WHO'S YOUR DADDY, NOW?"

But Albert didn't even listen for any of the answers floating up angrily from below. Instead, he directed his attention On High. "Hey, OLD MAN!" he yelled at God, "Look at me!! Roast your fattest pig and break out a jug, 'cause Albert Satcher's coming to dinner! YEE HAW!" The boys down on the ground looked on in stunned silence as Albert wiggled and danced on top of the pole, howling, "I AM THE MAN! THE MAN!!! THE MAN!!!"

In the book of Proverbs, Chapter 16, verse 18, it is written: "Pride goes before a fall." Albert stood there atop that pole, his hands reaching up into the heavens, when suddenly a great gust of wind struck him in the back. Arms pinwheeling, he fell forward. The wires, he thought, I'll grab the wires!! And he did. And they held. Albert hung there for a moment, thinking again how much these cables reminded him of snakes, when the very serpents that caught him bit hard. You see, friends, Fatty was wrong. The pole upon which Albert climbed that day did not hold telephone lines, no sir. I fear to tell you that the cables running along Old Pass Road, just south of Rose Hill, Mississippi, were high-tension powerlines.

On those snakelike cables, Albert hung, and the power surged through his small body. He shook violently back and forth, but the snakes wouldn't let go. His teeth rattled like coins in a wash drum, but the snakes wouldn't let go. His flesh began to crack and burn, but the snakes wouldn't let go. They bit and bit until, as suddenly as they had struck, they backed down. The surge stopped, and like Lucifer cast down from Heaven, so did Albert fall, a smoking wreck to earth. He landed amid the ragweed and dandelions, there on the side of the road, where his friends quickly surrounded him, ignoring the heat spilling from his body and the smell of burning hair. They shook his limp form and asked over and over again, "Albert, are you okay?" But our Albert knew of this not at all. For he was no longer there.

He awoke to a darkness utter and complete. But there was sound. It began as a single voice. Then there was another sound, joining the first. And then another. And then another. And with the addition of each voice, the darkness receded just a little, until Albert suddenly found himself no longer in darkness, but instead in a great white light. The chorus grew and grew, until Albert, dizzy with the sheer loveliness of the perfect song, fell to his knees and began shuffling forward, hoping beyond hope to find the source of the music. Time had no meaning, but there came a point when Albert, hands held before him as he inched forward, could not move any further. A barricade of some kind stood before him. Desperately opening his eyes against the brilliant light,

Albert could make out a gate towering above him. Reaching out his hands, the young boy began to push against the structure, and, to his delight, the gate began to move.

Then the music stopped.

A mighty voice rose like thunder. "ALBERT, YOUR ROOM HERE IS NOT YET READY."

The boy, in a fearful, high-pitched voice, replied, "But, Father, I don't care about a room. Please, let me stay with you. I can sleep anywhere."

"NO . . . YOU MUST GO! THERE IS MUCH FOR YOU TO DO."

"NOOOO!," Albert cried, but he was no longer before the gate. Instead, he found himself sitting in a white room on a bed surrounded by a host of machines making little clicking and whirring sounds. Blinking his eyes, he looked around. A glass of water rested on the nightstand beside the bed. Albert's tongue felt like some dead thing abandoned in the parched desert that once had been his mouth. Reaching for the glass, hoping to quench the fire burning in his throat, the boy soon realized that something about him had changed. For some reason he could not, no matter how hard he tried, reach the glass. The boy kept trying for several minutes, until, frustrated, he slammed his fists against the mattress . . . and missed. Looking down, amazed that he could actually swing and miss the bed, his breath stopped. His right and left arms were no longer there. Both ended just a little past his elbows. With a gasp, Albert fell back onto the bed, staring at the ceiling, letting it all sink in, and then, with a tortured howl, he began to cry.

He didn't notice the door open, but looked up when he felt a cool, slender hand fall upon his thigh. Sitting there beside him was an angel. Her eyes were dark and mysterious, and her lips were painted bright red. She was dressed all in white, and wore a strange hat, from beneath which a few auburn curls tried to escape.

"Are you from Heaven?" Albert marveled.

"No, dear," the woman smiled, "I'm from Memphis."

"What am I going to do?" Albert sobbed.

The lady from Memphis reached out her hand and caressed Albert's flushed cheek. "Let me show you something." The woman reached down beside the bed and lifted a cardboard box up on her lap. Reaching in, she pulled out two long flesh-colored cylinders. It appeared to Albert that the two were joined by a complex web of straps, and each cylinder ended in a disturbingly elegant silver hook.

"These are your new arms, my darling, and I promise you, if you work hard, if you learn how to use these really well, I think you'll be able to do anything you want."

And Albert did work hard. He learned how to do everything with his new arms. He learned how to dress himself. He learned how to feed himself. He learned how to write. But the most important thing Albert learned how to do with his new arms was to hold a book. Not any book, mind you. But THE BOOK. The Bible. For Albert had been touched by God. Within six months of Albert's release from the hospital in Meridian, Mississippi, the eleven-year-old's hair turned from rich ebony to platinum silver. And within nine months, Albert Satcher began to preach . . . standing in the streets of Jackson, telling all who passed about his journey to Heaven—and what waited for them beyond the gate. The young boy was no longer simply Albert Satcher. He was The Reverend Albert Satcher . . . touched by God, witness to Glory. He was THE MAN.

And the years passed. The world moved on, and so did Albert. He became known far and wide, preaching to churches, regardless of denomination, even as far away as Kentucky. He wasn't rich, but he was comfortable. Comfortable enough that on one Spring day in 1965 in Birmingham, Alabama, the Reverend Albert Satcher traded in his hooks for the finest artificial limbs money could buy. These arms had hands. Spring-loaded hands that could be operated ratchetlike by small tugs on the straps running from the arms and over Albert's shoulders. But the best thing about them, Albert thought, was that the metal hands were covered in flesh-colored rubber . . . so lifelike. They even had fingernails! Albert began wearing the arms constantly, and came to feel, for the first time in many years, whole.

That is, until one day, in 1975, when Albert was asked to speak to a small church in Valley Head, Alabama: Up and down the aisles of that Church, Albert loudly boomed. And he stood before his congregation at the pulpit, and hearts grew faint, as Albert led them into the light. His tongue was on fire, burning with the Holy Ghost. He raised his arms above his head, screaming hosannas at the rafters, and then looked to the organist, willing her to break into song.

He gasped. For there, sitting before the organ, was an angel looking back at him. She was the most beautiful creature he had ever seen. And for the second time in his life, Albert's heart stopped. He knew without a doubt that something was missing in his life, something that only the Heavenly Creature before him could fill. "God," he asked silently in his heart of hearts," I want that woman to be my wife. Please, God, please." But just as soon as Albert's request was made, from behind the woman's back a little boy's head peeked. For a moment, Albert almost rescinded his plea, but one more look at the woman's perfect cheekbones, her alabaster skin, the curve of her lips, and Albert let it go. He let it all go. "Okay, God, he can be my son."

The woman's name was Mary, my mother. And I was that little boy.

Albert would teach me the ways of God.

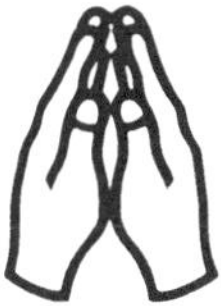

Toup Dreams

IN 1980 I MADE TWO BIG TRIPS, beloved, one following directly upon the other. The first ended when I completed my tenth lap around the sun; the second, well, the second occurred when my stepfather, the right Reverend Albert Satcher, woke up one day and announced over breakfast that the Good Lord had come to him in the night and suggested that it was time we moved south. Now, you must understand, we already lived south—Alabama South—and more precisely in a beautiful Eden called Will's Valley, a low country nestled between Sand and Lookout Mountain, two foothills of Appalachia. I remember my mother and I thinking it impossible to move to a latitude any lower, but we were not the type of people who ever took a suggestion from the Lord lightly, and within a week we were officially expelled from Paradise, the flaming sword at our back looking suspiciously like a Dairy Queen sign. Into the wilderness my family wandered, our destination unknown.

For poetic reasons, I wish I could tell you that we were lost for forty days and nights . . . but alas, our journey only lasted around forty hours, twelve of which were spent sitting in a motel room somewhere east of Birmingham. Through a maze of forgotten highways, and after having consumed a bounty of roadside manna (greasy potato wedges, pickled eggs, and a dead sea of

Coca-Cola), we entered a small town called Wadley . . . and there my second great journey of 1980 ended.

And the Vision began.

You see, my friends, when I describe our move from Will's Valley as an "Expulsion from Paradise," the analogy doesn't just end with our turning our backs on a landscape of unending loveliness and boundless freedom, and trekking into the wasteland of chickenhouses and stripmining that is Southern Alabama. No, I could only have wished that to be so. Instead, after my Dad found a flock in need of a shepherd (their pastor having been eaten alive by lymphatic cancer six months prior), we settled in a little trailer a mile and a half from the Church of The Lamb and Latter Signs. The chapel was a small white board structure that had been home to the Jehovah's Witnesses, the United Methodists, an unfortunate band of lost Mormons (who never had a chance, poor souls), and now . . . us. It took me only a few days to figure out that we had entered, truly, a land of banishment, a town so lifeless, slow, and mind-numbingly passive—clenched tightly in the grip of regulations, laws, and town ordinances—that I, a dullard even as nine-year-olds go, woke up on the third day of my incarceration there and exclaimed to my Mother, "I know where we are . . . this is the land of NOD!"

Yes, we were indeed lost in a desert of suburban humdrum, but don't fear, gentle reader, for, you know, there's something funny about deserts, about wastelands, whether they be real or imagined. Dreams seem to come more easily there . . . visions float more readily to the surface.

And, brother, did I ever find a vision.

TELEVISION.

I'm not saying that we were poor, my flock; we did own a TV back in Will's Valley, but there our little black-and-white RCA could pick up only one station, channel 3 out of Nashville, and then only if I forced my two-year-old brother Chris to lick his palm and gingerly hold the antennae. But in Wadley, just a few miles outside the bustling metropolis of Hackleburg, the signal was strong . . . and oh, my children, what eye-candy spilled from that 13-inch window! I was mesmerized by Laura Ingalls in *Little House on the Prairie,* captivated by Pinky Tuscadero on *Happy Days.* I believed wholeheartedly in the power of Steve Austin, that Six Million Dollar Man, and tearfully mourned the death of UltraMan. Everyday my world became bigger, but I would not truly experience unadulterated joy until one Sunday morning. At that time, my Granny Satcher was living with us, the arthritis in her back making it almost impossible for her to move without joint-searing pain, and she and I were sitting in the little front room of the trailer, both of us ignoring Albert's strained pleas for everyone to get ready for Church. She enjoyed television as much as I, and what made her such a treasured TV partner was that she would usually let me do all the picking, except on this particular day.

"E., turn over to station 10, Rev. Angley should be on . . ."

"Oh, Granny . . . ," I whined.

"Now just you do it, little man; don't you make me cut a switch!"

Pouting, as I was, and still am, prone to do, I flipped

over to channel 10. And there, my beloved flock, was a scene that forever changed my life.

Through the glass I watched, as a plump little man jumped and danced across a flower-strewn stage as if the Devil himself was riding his back. He wore a startling blue suit, and his hands, flying around his head like angry birds, glittered with rings of diamond and sapphire. His face was bright cherry-red, the top of his head crowned with a toupée as black as a sackcloth of hair. (Revelation 6:12) He screamed at his audience, saliva twinkling in the light as it rained from his mouth. What he was saying I didn't yet know, so consumed was I by the sheer spectacle. I fell to my knees watching as an old woman in a wheelchair was pushed up to the black-topped dynamo spinning across the stage. The preacher stopped moving, and the audience—a mêlée of hooping and hollering—became suddenly still. He looked like some great jungle cat as he gazed upon the frail little woman. There was power and electricity in the air, and suddenly the Reverend's fake hair, gaudy jewelry, and cheap suit, well, my children, it all just melted away. He touched the woman's forehead with the gentleness of a lover, and spoke in a voice as commanding as any general. "I RENOUNCE YOU SATAN! TAKE YOUR CLAWS OFF THIS WOMAN'S LEGS! GET BEHIND HER DEVIL! EVIL SPIRITS COME OWWWWT!!!" With a mighty push the woman's chair flew back, turning over, spilling her little body onto the stage, as if some great unseen hand had tossed her aside like a rag doll. Two men in black suits and sunglasses rushed to her side, obviously in an attempt to help her back into the chair, but before they came within a few feet, the woman leapt up, her hands clawing at the air. She began to dance, throwing her head back, singing joyfully, "I'M HEALED! I'M HEALED! I'M HEALED!" The camera then cut back to the squat little man, and he was just standing there, calm, knowing . . . all fire and ice, wind and rain.

I heard a creaking behind me, and reluctantly pulled my eyes away from the screen back to my Granny. She had climbed completely up out of her chair, standing as straight as a pin, all the pain of her joints seemingly forgotten. I'm telling you that in those brief few moments I saw before me not an old woman ravaged by the cruelty of time, but a lovely little girl, all pigtails and pink bows. She stared at the little television, and in the Sunday morning quiet, I heard her whisper:

"I love you . . . yes, I do."

† †

Isaiah 4:3 says that we should "Make straight in the desert a highway for God." A highway. Now, friends, and neighbors, I know about building roads. I worked on a Louisiana road crew the summer of 1989, and I can tell you that those shimmering ribbons that cut across our nation's landscape are made as much of sweat and tears as of tar and stone. The heat fries your brain, and the wind blows dust into every orifice, visible or not. Your boots fill up with sweat, gurgling with every step, and at the end of the day your hands look like they belong between two slices of bread, next to an order of potato salad. Beloved, my sermon today will focus on the men and women who toiled out there in the heat, whose broken backs and callused hands paved the way for many. I want to tell you about a road crew for God, and the highway to glory that they built. A road where God and man could meet, touch, and spark the birth of something new. Electric Revivalism! Televangelism!

On that heavenly crew, my friends, many worked, but a few stood out who would open the traditional camp revival to all segments of society, and pave the way for the coming of the television preacher. Before the arrival of these dedicated servants, the camp revival had been a sporadically occurring event, usually coinciding with a local miracle, and always locked away within regimented communities.

Into this traditional scenario came one Charles Finney, who was trained as a lawyer but gave up his practice after seeing God to become a Presbyterian minister in 1824. About ten years later, in 1835, Finney published his *Lectures on Revivals of Religion,* in which he instructed clergymen how to win at the great game of soul-saving. Quite simply, Finney proposed that "any means are acceptable in the war for humankind's soul." Brothers and Sisters, I don't know if you truly appreciate the scope of this little statement, but let me tell you that in one fell swoop, Charles Finney changed revivalism in America from an enterprise of passivity into a churning, burning machine of conversion. He proposed nothing less than a "technology" of revivalism, offering a radical new arsenal for young clergy intent on jumping into the Great War against the Devil. Finney suggested that churches set aside periods of time in which all regular and sacred activities would stop as churchgoers fully devoted themselves to large "prayer meetings," oftentimes concentrating on a particular theme. He believed that women should have an active leadership role in the church, and that all those who "felt the call" should preach whether they were ordained or not. He adamantly suggested that ministers begin to use a more dramatic, vigorous style of preaching in order to impress their congregations. Intent on drowning the stoic, fearful nature of Calvinism, with its ideology that all things in Creation are pre-ordained and only an elect few will be saved, Finney opened the floodgates for all to follow.

Yes, beloved, Finney wrote the text and designed the machine, but it was his successor Dwight Moody who built it and made it run. Moody's career began just after the Civil War and lasted until the end of the nineteenth century, a time when the economy in America changed from a small market to a vast empire. The difference, beloved, is that a traditional business in the earlier market economy was a "single-unit" operation as opposed to an emerging form of enterprise that consists of a hierarchy of salaried executives and many distinct operating units running simultaneously. In other words, the haberdashery was transformed into the department store. Moody, a product of his time, likewise transformed Finney's entrepreneurial revivalism into a full fledged enterprise, thereby inventing a grand, urban-centered form of revivalism.

This organizational change made it possible to reach

increased numbers of people. In effect, it mass-produced salvation. Before a revival would take place, Moody would send his staff into the area, make financial connections, talk to the locals, and begin preliminary events that would spark interest and excitement among them. He would talk to a number of preachers, carefully selecting the most outspoken, outrageous, and popular, and invite them to preach at his event. He instructed his staff to enter people's homes to preach in their kitchens, dens, and dining rooms. Like Finney, Moody believed that the preacher should use any means possible to move people on down the road to Glory, and his legacy is to have shaped urban revivalism into a truly popular religion for the masses. In essence, Moody created "The God Biz." Its product . . . eternal life for all.

So, friends, if we have a manifesto written by Finney, and a war machine mobilized by Moody, then all we're lacking is the most important part. Beloved, the gears of war must always be greased with flesh and blood . . . there must be someone willing to fight in the trenches. A soldier. As Moody's era was drawing to a close, yet another extraordinary man stepped forward to challenge the forces of darkness; he went by the name Billy Sunday. Once a professional baseball player, Sunday received his calling in 1896. Within a short period of time, he would become Mr. Showmanship of revivalists and single-handedly complete the popularization of the religious institution within American culture.

Above all, Sunday knew how to *sell.* A master storyteller, he relied on dramatic entertainment to enthrall his audience. If he were telling the story of Naaman the leper washing himself in the Jordan to cleanse away his sores, for example, the evangelist would reënact the scene before his congregation: slapping at imaginary fleas, shivering at the cold of the water, comically stubbing his toe on the rocks. Crowds would roll with laughter as Sunday would imitate a society woman cradling her pug dog, a drunk stumbling out of a saloon, or an effeminate minister examining his nails before getting behind the pulpit. He would skip, run, dance, and gyrate across the stage. He would rage against the Devil, often going so far as picking up a chair sitting by the pulpit and smashing it into kindling. He would illustrate the idea of a sinner trying to reach Heaven by acting like a ballplayer sliding into home plate—running full speed and throwing himself across the entire length of the stage. Sunday was outspoken; he was controversial; he was a superstar. In our little history, he brings us to the brink of the television era, the last great personality to influence revivalism without the aid of broadcasting.

Then, in November 1928, on a cold Wednesday evening in New York, a voice would forever change the face of religious expression in America. It wasn't loud. It wasn't dazzling. In fact, it flowed like cold molasses from radios across Manhattan. From radio station WLWL, there entered into the rough and tumble town of broadcasting a stranger. Luckily, this outsider didn't ride alone. God watched his back. His name was Bishop Fulton J. Sheen.

At the time, the future of Fulton's radio program, *The Catholic Hour,* looked grim. Considered to be "filler" by the owners of WLWL, who unhappily relinquished to pressure placed on them by influential members of the local diocese, Fulton's show was given the worst possible time-slot. The station believed that the church and its supporters would slink quietly away, once the program failed. But with all of the cards stacked against him, Fulton Sheen walked forward like a classic Greek hero. Like Ulysses, Fulton bravely sailed down an unknown river, flanked on one side by the mighty Amos and Andy, and on the other by the titan vaudevillian Fred Allen. Only one could leave the fray victorious.

A mighty battle ensued. In a matter of two weeks, *The Catholic Hour* was the highest rated radio program in New York. In another two weeks, the show went national. Years passed, and the Bishop's program appeared to be unstoppable. He truly was a gunslinger, shooting down the Devil at every turn. One would think that things could not get any better for the Good Bishop, that is, until Fulton was given the opportunity of a lifetime. In 1950, our hero was approached by a commercial television network, and, undaunted by the Beast, he accepted. The Bishop's TV program, also entitled *The Catholic Hour*, entered the race slowly, but by 1952 it was drawing a high share of the evening television audience, even without the lavish flourishes demonstrated by many of its competitors. The show's production values were humble by any stretch of the imagination: Fulton's only crew was a cameraman who doubled as a stagehand; his set consisted of a desk, a chair, and a blackboard; no TelePrompTers were used; the show was completely unrehearsed. It thoroughly baffled everyone. And no religious program since has consistently drawn the audience it enjoyed between 1950 and 1954. Bishop Sheen single-handedly paved the road for the televangelical convoy that followed.

Beginning in the mid nineteen fifties and early sixties, television swarmed with an entire generation of evangelists who went on to create incredibly far-reaching religious organizations: Dwight Moody's dream made incarnate. Oral Roberts, having for years held revival and healing services throughout the South, aired his first television broadcast in 1954. Today, he presides over a multimillion-dollar organization which includes Oral Roberts University and the City of Faith complex in Tulsa, Oklahoma. In 1956, Jerry Falwell, just out of Bible College, began broadcasting from a former Donald Duck juice-bottling building in Lynchburg, Virginia. Today, he is the outspoken voice of the Moral Majority, founder of a liberal-arts college in Virginia, and his television program *The Old Time Gospel Hour* (filmed in the large Thomas Road Baptist Church) is watched weekly by millions. Pat Robertson, trained as a lawyer, but having repeatedly failed to pass the bar exam, purchased a defunct television station in Virginia Beach in 1960 with a vision to establish the first religious television station. From this dream, the Christian Broadcasting Network was born. Headquartered in Virginia Beach, CBN is best known for its flagship program *The 700 Club,* but also owns four television stations, six radio stations, a recording company, a news network, a university, and a satellite earth station. Robert Schuller began his ministry in 1955. Spending his last dime to buy an organ, his first service was held in a drive-in theater, with Schuller preaching from the roof of the snack bar. Today, he preaches from the Crystal Cathedral, the $15-million glass sanctuary of the Garden Grove Community Church, and can be seen weekly on his television program *The Hour of Power.*

From the nineteen fifties through the turmoil of the sixties, past the seventies, eighties, and nineties, and now into the twenty-first century, the list of television evangelists grows ever longer. James Robison, Jimmy Swaggart (the largest selling gospel-music recording artist of all time), Kenneth and Gloria Copeland, Jan and Paul Crouch (TBN), Benny Hinn, Creflo and Taffi Dollar, Mark Finey *(It Is Written),* Mother Angelica, Jack and Rexella Van Impe: These are all men and women who have followed in the legacy of Finney, Moody, and Sunday, democratizing salvation by allowing every person the opportunity to drink from the fount of redemption, regardless of class, physical mobility, race, or gender. Four fundamentalist "networks" keep broadcast dishes aimed at fixed-orbit satellites, bouncing programs over the continent twenty-four hours a day. Competing evangelists buy $600 million worth of radio and television time a year. At last count, the United States had 1,400 all-gospel radio stations and about 30 gospel television stations. Instead of revival tents, we now have Astrodomes. There is no limit to the resources the media offers . . . even our own Ernest Angley runs his ministry from a $2.5-million cathedral in Akron, Ohio, complete with 24-karat gold veneered pulpit and piano, crystal chandeliers, a red-lit "fountain of blood," and side-by-side pictures of himself and Jesus, painted on black velvet. The cathedral is dedicated to Rev. Angley's wife, who died many years ago of ulcerative colitis and is buried beneath a twenty-three-foot-high, twenty-ton marble angel on the church lawn.

Yes, they all have been successful in the ways of the world.

† †

Brothers and Sisters, when I told some friends that I intended to preach on televangelists, I noticed how their faces clenched, how their eyes fell. Over and over, I was asked how I would treat the subject: How could I say anything positive? Don't TV ministers take money from the aged, sick, and infirm, and then buy private airplanes and build fancy glass churches with the proceeds? Are they anything more than lying hypocrites? My children, it is not my place to judge. I am well familiar with all of the horror stories. I remember in 1978 when the chess champion Bobby Fisher accused the Rev. Garner Ted Armstrong of using mind control to bilk him out of $100,000. I remember the falls of Jim Bakker and Jimmy Swaggart. Even recently, I laughed in horror at the rantings of Jerry Falwell, as he set out to attack the little Teletubby, Tinky Winky. But beloved, I have never allowed myself to forget that they are all, in the end, simply men; not God, but simple instruments of Grace.

Just a few weeks ago, on a Saturday afternoon, I was lazily flipping through the channels and paused on PBS, channel 10 in Las Vegas. Playing was a documentary that I had seen a number of years ago, entitled *Hoop Dreams.*

For those of you unfamiliar, my lambs, the film follows four years in the life of two young men in Chicago who want to follow in their hero Isiah Thomas's footsteps and one day play professional basketball. At the very beginning of the film, we look into the living rooms of Arthur Agee and William Gates and watch as they gaze longingly, lovingly, into their televisions, entranced by a game and drowning in the image of Isiah as he lopes across the court. There is a fire there burning in their eyes, my friends . . . a fire of passion that anyone who has every really wanted something, ever really needed something, understands. It is the thirst of unquenchable desire. It is the spark that drives all engines of aspiration.

When I looked at them, when I watched their story, I was immediately whisked back to that trailer in Wadley, Alabama, where a nine-year old boy was mesmerized by a rotund little man who moved across the stage with all the power and grace of Doctor J or Magic Johnson. The news is filled each week with the soap-opera antics of the Allen Iversons, the Latrell Sprewells, and the Dennis Rodmans of the multimillion-dollar basketball industry. But, beloved, when you see them move down that court, when you are witness to the grace and power of that round-ball ballet, then you cannot deny that, if only briefly, all is forgiven. When those men soar through the air, defying gravity, you know that you are witness to a miracle, and for a flash you forget your problems, you forget your pains, you are transfigured by the simple joy of the spectacle.

Brothers and Sisters, there have been many times

when it would have been easy for me to lose my faith in the men and women who evangelize over the airwaves. It seems to me that the feelings of doubt and distrust are as much a part of human nature as is the desire to eat or make love. But in the end, all those feelings do is leave us tired and alone, warming the bench, watching others as they move across the court. My friends, there comes a time when you have to get in the game, when you have to run down the court, and when, faced by the demonic defense of disbelief, rise up with the wings of eagles. (Isaiah 40:31) My children, every moment of our lives must be Jordanesque leaps of faith! I took my first on a Sunday morning some twenty years ago. I watched an old woman stand before me, her hurt gone, her eyes clear, the crisp promise of love on her lips. I watched her, leapt bravely with her into the unknown, and in that void of the human heart I was changed forever. I didn't yet have any idea about the rules of the game, and I certainly didn't know whether or not I had a chance at winning. I still don't know whether I'll truly be able to fill that toupée, but I knew that my destiny lay there on that stage, the power of God behind me and the mystery of humanity before me. I stood on the line, friends, took my shot, and discovered, in one bright, shining moment, that God rang true in the nature of one rug-wearing preacher named Ernest Angley.

And for that moment, Ernest, I am in your debt.
May God Bless You.

The Straight or Crooked Way

IF ANY OF YOU HAVE SEEN me lately, my congregation, you may have noticed that my face has cracked wide open. Separating the top and bottom is a great split that one could not describe so much as a smile, but more a toothy chasm of joy. In fact, beloved, the corners of my mouth are so far apart, it wouldn't surprise me if the top of my head slid clean off. Reverend, you ask, why can't you restrain yourself? Pastor, Why can't you just calm down and sit still! Please . . . think of the children!

Well, I'm here to tell you that there'll be no calming down. I'm here to tell you there'll be no sittin' pretty. I'm saying, yank up those little porch monkeys by the ears, and point them in this direction, Halleluiah!, because friends and neighbors, the Good Lord has gone and set off an M-80 of joy inside my head, Glory to God, and I intend to get a little glop of happy on all those around me. Praise Be!

So what's done it? I mean, Lord knows I have my blue days like everyone else, but overall I'm a happy sort. A good egg, as my Mamaw used to say, but this eyes a'rollin', hands a'shakin' kind of ecstasy is something new. Don't get me wrong, now, beloved, that happiness *is* on occasion chemically induced: Hershey's chocolate, Thousand Island Dressing, Pringle's potato chips . . . just throw in that Fox show *V.I.P.*, and my head's dragging under

Heaven's basement. But this time is different. You see, my lambs, lately, well, I've been hearing something. It started not long ago. I'd be walking around the house and suddenly stop, thinking that I could hear a cat crying. I would search the rooms, but never find the source. It sure wasn't my own big tom, Cookie, always sprawled corpse-like on my desk. As the weeks passed, I kept hearing the sound, beginning to suspect that this was more than just some love-stricken feline . . . the noise was just too darn painful.

Finally, I knew.

That sound was coming from a lot lower than under my house, sweet neighbors. A LOT LOWER. This was a cry echoing from the great void, from the Stygian darkness. It was a cry of mind-shattering pain.

You see, friends, that old Devil, well, he's a little under the weather right now. To be more precise, just lately he's been feeling about as low as a snake in a gully. Deep hurting, as the commercial used to say. Deep and sure and to the quick. And nothing, I mean nothing, could make me happier!

Why is he SOOO in pain? You do ask a lot of questions, friends, but I promise I won't hold anything back from you. The Devil's hurting because High Art has come to Las Vegas!

Hell, my friends, has frozen over!

† †

If you were to drive up Las Vegas Boulevard in the Fall of 1998, brethren, and come to the site where once stood the fabulous Dunes Hotel and Casino, you would have seen that the desert soil spewed forth something new and wonderful. As you will learn, well, something a peson may even call miraculous. Now, I'm not going to beat around the bush, because you all know what I'm talking about. Yes, yes, I know, if there's something new in Las Vegas, you're thinking that there must be some cards, dice, and silicon somewhere in the mix. But THIS, my friends, woooieeee, it just ain't your Daddy's casino. This is the Bellagio Resort and Casino. For a while, you couldn't watch twenty minutes of TV without hearing some of that Italian opera bellowing out of the screen, accompanied by the sight of a pretty girl with sweet, billowing hair in her eyes. Praise the Lord, every time that commercial came on, I wanted to squeeze my wife with one hand, and shovel Chef Boyardees into my mouth with the other: The hype for this place was thicker than Tennessee molasses in February, and about as cloying.

Even I, friends and neighbors, began having dreams of Versace and Chanel. And with those dreams, those nightmares, something twisted occurred inside my chest. It started when I heard that on the walls of this Babylon would be paintings . . . great paintings. I became cynical. You heard me. A thick wall closed around my heart like a caul, and I was determined that anything dressing itself all fancy like that, well, it must be the spawn of Satan. I was weak, Brothers and Sisters, and in my frailty, like I often do, I took the easy path. Old Mr. Steve Wynn, the proprietor of this new palace, couldn't really care about all that art, could he? He was just some rich man, I told myself . . . what could he know about true passion, true vision? Like the Bible says, it's easier for a camel to pass through the eye of a needle, than for a rich man to enter the kingdom of heaven. (Matthew 19:24). I mean, we all know that little rich boys are more concerned with their WAD, not GOD, right? How could someone be truly inspired if they don't know God? And, desperate in my poverty, I was like a jealous child, refusing to share my Father's love with someone just because his plastic was of a different color. Heck, I don't even have any plastic. Do you see what I was doing, brethren? I was refusing to take a chance. I was living in Las Vegas, but refusing to gamble—not on cards, but on the nature of one man.

That jealous fear, biting down on my heart like some raging Hell beast, finally was washed away, my children, one night when I found myself preaching in front of the newly opened casino. I had wanted to get to the Luxor, but due to construction, and some wrong turns, I instead landed outside the lion's den itself. I decided to take my chances. Hellfire and brimstone burned in my mouth, and I raged against the storm that I swore loomed just on the horizon. I screamed, I say I SCREAMED for Mr. Steve Wynn to show himself, to come on out. Then, as I looked across the big, beautiful lake out front to the twinkling lights of the casino, the angelic voice of Frank Sinatra rose in song, and, Glory to God, a great wall of water sprang 250-feet into the air. THE MAN had stepped in, beloved, and the wind carried a great gusher splashing against my face. I sputtered, and the crowd laughed at me. They laughed and laughed, and something changed in my heart. I looked out across the majesty of that fountain, and, hacking up a little more of Lake Mead, I also began to laugh. I walked up to the entrance of Bellagio, still chuckling, surrounded by people. Just as Old Blue Eyes finished *Luck Be A Lady,* I entered, and within a few hours I knew . . . I understood. All was not lost, a turning point had been reached.

Regardless of his fancy suits, regardless of the depths of his pockets, I knew that the Grace of God had moved one Steven A. Wynn, Halleluiah, moved him into a crossroads. He had been given the greatest of God's gifts, the permission, I say, the permission to choose his own path, and, Glory to God, I would soon come to believe that he had chosen wisely.

† †

There are two roads, Brothers and Sisters, two roads that lead from Valley Head, Alabama. One is an Interstate, built during the Johnson Administration, as straight and black as a coachwhip. The other road is old Mt. Pass, a winding pothole that always leaves your jaw sore and temper short. However, both roads lead to the same place . . . Gadsden. To many of you, I dare say, all of you, the name Gadsden, Alabama doesn't set your spine a'tinglin' or your backside a'rockin'. But, my friends, to a ten-year-old country boy from Valley Head with a little spending cash, Gadsden was a place where dreams came true. You see, just off the Interstate between Birmingham and Chattanooga at Exit No. 123, between a Krystal Burger and the Texaco, there lay a testament to all things great and prosperous in America: Wal-Mart. Filled with just about everything a mortal heart could desire, it was a treasure trove, and also a window to what lay outside the borders of DeKalb County. It was the Vegas of my childhood. At the registers were racks and racks of magazines, the shelves were lined with exotic foods, and the fabrics were of colors and designs that spoke of faraway places with strange sounding names. Plus, they sold guns and Moonpies. A store can't be half bad if you can eat a Moonpie while buying ammunition.

None of this mattered to me, though, in that Summer of 1981. Only one thing of any importance existed amid all that glitter, and, beloved, I would never call her a thing. Her name was Apollonia. I had first seen her on my best friend Steven Hawkins's closet door, and the moment I had looked into her soulful eyes, I knew that one day we would be together. The poster was almost life-size, and Steven said it had been expensive, but she was worth it. Brethren, the very next day I began to pool my money. In a week of odd-jobs, I had enough, and, since our car was on the fritz, I knew that my Aunts Lilla and Alice were the only hope of reaching this, my ultimate goal.

Now, the problem was which one to ask. Alice was a fast driver, but liked sissy-sounding music, plus her car was always about twenty degrees hotter than hell, Praise Be! Lilla, on the other hand, didn't even have a radio in her car, preferred the windows down, and always had candy in her purse. But, Brothers and Sisters, she was slow . . . so very slow. Dogs could run lazy loops around her Ford when she went down Highway 11. And, when she went to Gadsden, she always took Mt. Pass, and always, I say always, stopped to take a jar of preserves to Miss

Willie Davenport, an old black woman who lived halfway between Valley Head and Gadsden: Miss Willie had been a widow for twenty-five years, but her face was ageless; only hair as white as snow offered any clues to the number of spins Willie had taken around the sun. In the end, I decided I would take my chances with Alice. Sometimes a man just had to be a man, I thought, and no amount of musical horror, not even a desert of blinding heat, would stand between me and my Apollonia.

On the morning we were to go, I sprang from my bed, and ran down the stairs, expecting to see Aunt Alice already dressed and ready. But instead, who sat at the breakfast table, driving gloves pulled tightly over her spidery fingers? Lilla. "I told Alice I would take you," she said. "Miss Willie's niece is staying with her for a few weeks, and I want you to play with her and make her feel welcome. That's my boy, grab a biscuit and let's go, I want to be back by dark." Soon, we were winding snakelike through the elms and poplars lining Mt. Pass. For the entire ride to the Davenport farm I fumed, boiling over like a forgotten kettle. When we pulled into the driveway, Lilla got out, came around to the passenger door, opened it and gave me a look that—well, brethren, I remember a boyhood myth about a cockatrice, a beast that could turn you to stone with one look. To this day, I think Lilla was one part cockatrice, because some of her looks, I swear, could sour milk. I marched behind her into the house. Miss Willie squeezed me tightly, and after pinching every inch of my face, pushed me toward the back door. "Sonya's out in the back, so you git along, little man. Laws, you a sweet one!"

Miss Willie was so excited that when we reached the back door, she gave me an energetic slap. With a scream, I fell down the backsteps into the yard, fell face first into the grass, but when I looked up . . . well, Brothers and Sisters, I fell again. For as I raised my head, before my eyes stood the prettiest girl I had ever seen. She stood there in a white dress, her hair done up in pigtails tied with pink ribbon. I just never knew angels would fly so close to the ground. She had been watering Miss Willie's flowers with a garden hose, but at that moment held the hose before her, brandishing it like a gun. She didn't look surprised . . . just thoughtful. "You fell pretty hard; are you okay?" she asked. I stammered an affirmative. She smiled, "Well, your face is pretty dirty, I guess you should probably wash up." I didn't have time to speak, before a blast of water struck me full force in the face. Friends, I was in love.

It was late in the afternoon when we arrived at Wal-Mart. I remember the whole world seemed a little brighter. When we went into the store, Lilla and I decided to meet back at the car when we were done. An hour later, when I slid into the seat of the Ford, I held a little bag in my hands. "Lord, that must be a stamp, not a poster, boy," Lilla laughed. I smiled and told her that I had changed my mind, and asked if we could stop back at the Davenports for just a minute on the way home.

What was in that bag, friends? Well, I'm here to tell you, the price of an Apollonia poster buys a lot of pink ribbons.

† †

So, beloved, I walked from the fountains into the main lobby of Bellagio, my face still damp from the spray. I imagine I looked like a deer in the headlights. I stumbled through the casino, beneath a large, garish chandelier by that master glass artist Dale Chihuly, and into a great arboretum. In the center of all that glass and steel towered a massive 30-foot-tall Horn of Plenty, made of a plethora of flowers, the colors so shocking that my eyes watered. I walked around this garden and entered the Gallery of Fine Art, pushing through the line, ignoring the curses and angry stares. Steve Wynn had two roads from which to choose, the straight or crooked way. I had to see. Glory to God, I had to know which one he would take.

I looked at the tomblike marble space, the men in dark suits looming in the corners, the lines of people waiting to get in, and then the paintings, the sculptures. Twenty-five works graced the somber rooms. There, on the right, the exquisite *Portrait of Paul Guillaume* by Amedeo Modigliani. In the center, as perfect a Giacometti as I have ever seen, his *Man Pointing*. To the left, the beautiful *Flag on Orange Field II* by a man named Jasper Johns. All the works glowed in an otherworldly light, windows looking into other worlds, other times, faraway places with strange-sounding names. I looked at the mix of joy and awe on the faces of the men and women who wandered within the hushed interior. Finally, in a moment of divine inspiration, I knew. Glory to God, I knew. This, brethren, was much more than a casino, this was much more than a simple art collection. This was a wake. A glorious wake, beloved, to bid our farewells to the spirits of these great dead works. Before the entrance of the marble tomb in which they lie is a massive pile of sweet flowers. Friends, look, their tomb is surrounded by respectful pallbearers in dark suits. A line of people files through the darkness, quietly whispering their good-byes before exiting back into the light where they will dance, and sing, and gamble.

I told you that Mr. Wynn had been given the right to choose, beloved, and as I stood in that joyous tomb, I knew that Steve had done right. I envisioned the Devil coming in the dark of night to Steve's bed and whispering, "Hey Steve, hey buddy old pal, c'mon, who's gonna come to this town, *my* town, to look at a bunch of girlie paintings? Listen, my man, what you need in Bellagio is a roller coaster, or better yet, just ditch the whole Italian crap and go with the Titanic as a theme . . . I can hook you up with my friend Cameron as soon as tomorrow." Well, loved ones, do you know what Steve said when confronted by that wily old serpent? He screamed, damnation, "GET BEHIND ME, DEVIL." Yes, the Devil offered him the easy road, but moved by God, Steven A. Wynn made his highway the hard way. He rebuked the mediocrity of theme parks and Hollywood memorabilia, turning his sharp, all-seeing eyes to the light of truth. Yes, neighbors, I'm here to tell you that the Bellagio could easily have been Steve's Apollonia, a fool's dream, all slick and pretty, made up like a whore. But when the time came to choose, Steve chose Sonya; he chose all of us. Flesh over paper, substance over style. Halleluiah!

I left with a glad heart. Steve Wynn was a man with a vision, and the courage to make it a reality. Sure, sure, he had a lot of help. A host of high-powered art dealers, critics, and advisors were enlisted to scale the walls of the art-world's battlements, and, ladies and gentlemen, without a dear member of our own congregation, Libby Lumpkin, the tough and exceedingly lovely gallery curator, well, The Bellagio Gallery of Fine Art would have been just a house of cards awaiting a demonic blow. Puff, all gone. But a tiny bit of uncertainty still tickled the back of my mind. For, Brothers and Sisters, a wake must end. Had Mr. Wynn taken this into account? Did he realize that a wake has nothing to do with the dead, for they have moved on, but is about the living and those who must go on? Believers don't fear death, only the wicked (Proverbs 10:24). These questions plagued my mind.

My answer would come a week later when I returned once more, Brothers and Sisters. I know not what drove me back. Perhaps I wanted to say one more good-bye. Maybe that doubt still wasn't completely gone. Well, beloved, earlier I mentioned that something miraculous had happened in Las Vegas, and now I'm going to tell you what that was. When I entered the gallery, I immediately knew something had changed. It took a few minutes for my eyes to adjust, but as soon as they did, I almost fell to my knees. Glory to God, a lot of the work was gone . . . I mean a lot. Sold to a higher bidder, I assumed. Good-bye, *Man Pointing*. You will be greatly missed, *Flag on Orange Field II*. Farewell, Constantin Brancusi's *Mademoiselle Pogany II*, you will always hold a special place in my heart. And *Clothespin* by Claes Oldenburg, well, I never got to know you as well as I should have. In that moment of revelation, my friends, it all became clear to me. Like Jesus rising from his tomb to disappear into the heavens, Mr. Wynn's great art vanished back into the public realm, only to be replaced by the hope for still more to come.

In the desert, God has bestowed visions on many men and women. Only now it is time for those visions, in particular those artistic visions of a purely secularized world, to be returned into the lifeblood of humanity. My loved ones, Steve Wynn was that Heavenly Postman. He brought the dead to Las Vegas for all to say good-bye, leaving us to continue our play. Today, Steve Wynn has left the Bellagio behind, but his crusade is far from over. Many have taken up his cause, and, through their collective efforts, high art has found itself a niche in the land of sex and sin. Yes, beloved, Steve Wynn was a visionary, and his vision was true only because, for a brief time, he was as a boy filled with childlike wonder, bearing a bag of pink ribbons. He turned away from the straight paths of his contemporaries, and wandered the long and crooked road where beauty still walks among the sycamores. I think she wears a pretty white dress. God has blessed you, Steve Wynn, and allowed you to do nothing less than raise the dead—a miracle for all to behold, and a blessing for living artists who gamble each and every day, and walk in the shining light of God.

Ashes to Ashes. Dust to Dust. Amen.

A Wedding at the Sistine Chapel

[a revised version of a ceremony performed in Vatican City on March 25, 2001, with Robert Millar and Holly Knight]

HOLLY AND ROBERT, I want you to hold hands and snuggle up close to me. That's it . . . come in real tight, so we can whisper.

I don't know about you, but I'm scared. I feel like I've got these icy fingers tickling my back. I just don't know where I am, you see. Or, more precisely, I just can't believe that I am where it appears I am, if you catch my drift. I know, I'm not making a lot of sense, but listen, the last thing I remember, I was sitting in San Antonio, Texas, trying to get the lid off of some strawberry preserves. Now, suddenly, here I am, standing with the two of you, packed shoulder to shoulder in a big room, squeezed together like cattle, and, you know what, I don't think any of these people speak English. I've heard about stuff like this on that paranormal late-night radio talk show, *Coast to Coast A.M. with Art Bell.* The story is always the same . . . some redneck like me is sitting out in Podunk, USA, trying to open a jar of strawberry preserves, when all of a sudden he is whisked away in a bright light, shown amazing sights, and then, to his dismay, PROBED. My gosh, it even happened to Ezekiel. (Ezekiel 1:1-28) Well, my lambs, I most definitely have been whisked away. I have not yet been probed (although those guys at the exit, with the black coats, look like they would be more than happy to provide this service), but every time I look up I see a sight so amazing, so preposterous, that I know this must be one of those abductions Mr. Bell talks about—or at the very least, something must have gone seriously wrong with the strawberry preserves I had been eating.

Because up there, over our heads, do you see it? Heck, you can't miss it. It's a painting that covers the whole ceiling. And if that painting is real, and not just some cosmic joke cooked up by our good neighbors from Rinok 6, then the three of us must be standing together in—
and I can barely get my mind around this possibility—
The Sistine Chapel.

What? Robert, Holly, tell this man that it isn't wise to try laying a mind-fiddle on a Man of God. You are kidding me. This is REAL? We are in the Vatican, and the two of you brought me here to marry you beneath the glorious ceiling of the Cappella Sistina? Oh, please forgive me, my children, it's all coming back to me now. I have spent countless hours being accosted by the demons of Air France, I fear that I have tried to block out much. Hmmmm. Let's see. Okay, all together now, let's shuffle over to our right, and tie this knot up good and tight, Italian-style.

Here we are. Look up above us, there. See that panel? It is called "The Creation of the Stars and Planets," and it reminds me of something else I heard on the Art Bell show. There were these astronomers on the air, arguing about God's Universe, and one of the fellas started talking about this phenomenon called a Binary Star. Ever heard of it? Well, according to this scientist, under certain conditions two stars may be formed from the chaos of molecular clouds and forever married in a manner that causes them to dynamically engage with each other throughout the balance of their lives. They spin and revolve and dance. Blessed Jesus, how they dance, held firmly in an embrace of ultimate attraction! As they promenade through the eons, their union strengthens: dancing together, united forever, in perfect order, born from chaos.

My two friends, you are very much like those stars. And today, in this Chapel, beneath the Genesis painted by Michelangelo way back in 1510, we celebrate the genesis of your union, your choice to spend eternity together, your hearts made one in the furnace of this great passion that you feel for one another. Amen.

May we pray.

"Oh Lord our God, source of all Blessing, in happiness and joy, I thank you for these two people. May you give Holly and Robert the ability to rejoice always in their love for one another. May you fulfill every wish of their hearts. May you open their eyes to the beauty and mystery of the love they hold for each other, every day as today. And may their life together embrace and nurture the promise of this moment, so that all who know them will call them blessed. Amen."

Now, my children, in turn, I want you to take the rings that you have brought with you across so many miles, and place them on the ring finger of one another's left hand. Good. Don't be shy, Robert. There you go. The wedding ring is a symbol of the unbroken unity of truth that from this point forward will represent your marriage. St. Augustine writes: "The nature of God is like a circle whose center is everywhere and circumference cannot be found." May these rings forever represent the vows you make to one another this day.

Holly, if you will repeat after me . . .

"I promise, Robert, that my love for you will be as timeless as the beauty of this Chapel. I vow, my love, to forever respect who you are, to stand by you throughout all of life's changes, and to nurture and strengthen the love between us, for as long as we both shall live."

And Robert, please repeat these words . . .

"I promise, Holly, that my love for you will be as timeless as the beauty of this Chapel. I vow, my love, to forever respect who you are, to stand by you throughout all of life's changes, and to nurture and strengthen the love between us, for as long as we both shall live."

Oh, Glory to God, my friends . . . I hear the wonder in your voices, the truth in your words. Robert and Holly, I want you to walk out of this Chapel today, out into the majesty of Rome, and know that from this day forth all is new. You will never be alone. You will always be ONE. I feel such excitement for the bright and wonderful future that you will share together. Of course, there will be dark times. Holly, don't pay any attention to that panel over on the left, showing Judith cutting off Holofernes head. Robert, cover your eyes when you pass beneath that section showing a drunken Noah trying to lose himself in so much grape goodness. I want you both, beloved, to know that no darkness can overwhelm the light that you hold for one another in your hearts. Together, there is nothing you cannot do.

I spoke earlier of feverish dreams brought on by bad fruit. I wish for you still more feverish dreams . . . the hot, impassioned dreams that will forever drive you deeply into one another's arms, and thus, into the Glory of God's perfect embrace.

I now pronounce you husband and wife. What God has joined together, let no one put asunder. You may kiss, hold each other close, and never let go. Amen.

Virtual Heaven

FOR SOME TIME, actually my whole life, Brothers and Sisters, I have been desperately waiting for a certain event . . . the ultimate pleasure cruise and resort destination combo, if you will.

In the Bible, it is called the Rapture . . . a path to Heaven. At the turn of the last millennium, I, your simple pastor, experienced stronger and stronger visions of riding up into the sky, dancing among the stars, and entering through the gates of Paradise. I know, I know . . . no living soul can possibly predict when the end times will occur. Only God knows these things, as it says in Isaiah 46. But, beloved . . . I WANTED IT!!! I NEEDED IT!!! As December 31, 1999 approached, my desk became cluttered with books filled with prophecies. I read and reread the Books of Daniel and Revelation. Words upon words upon words . . . the images coursing like an unstoppable river through my mind, washing the world away. Friends would call to wish me "Merry Christmas," but I no longer heard them, no longer listened. All I heard were the words of Paul, and his promise that I would, on the Day of Translation, rejoin with my resurrected body, fly up to meet Jesus in the air, and swirl away before the face of God forever and ever. (1 Thessalonians 4:16-17) I was ready; I was willing; my dance card was open and my suit was pressed . . . but, with less than one week left in the twentieth century, I just didn't feel like my dream date with God was confirmed.

It was early Tuesday morning, December 28, 1999, as I sipped coffee, watched television, and nibbled at a little raspberry tart, when I realized that my apocalyptic experience felt just a little hollow. Pride began to burn brightly in my heart, and the Devil whispered seductively in my ear: "Hey! Buuuuuddeeeeeee! DUDE (for some reason I can't fathom, the devil sounded suspiciously like Pauly Shore), all these other guys got a vision . . . why not you? Look, Ethan, at that Jack Van Impe on the TV. He's so smug. Why, I bet all the writers of those books on your desk, I bet THEY got visions. You know what I think, huh? I think the Old Man is giving you the . . ."

The Devil didn't get the chance to finish, for at that moment, brethren, I began to choke on a particularly nasty bit of pastry, and, spilling my coffee, I knocked a stack of books onto the floor. As I reached down to pick them up, I noticed one was open, lying beside a semi-crumpled pamphlet. I had found the book—*The Spiritual Diary,* by Emanuel Swedenborg—on an evangelical trip to Stockholm just a month ago. It lay open to an illustration of Heaven, depicting a beautiful city perched high upon a mountain, surrounded by gardens, hovering above a great human city. The pamphlet, with part of its cover missing, was brought back by the Rev. Mrs. from one of her recent trips to Los Angeles; it was entitled "Architecture & Gardens: A Tour," and on its cover was shown a graceful stone structure rising above a beautiful garden. I looked quickly from one image to the other, back and forth, back and forth, and suddenly, beloved, my heart soared! For here was my promised vision . . . here was my preview of Paradise. On the cover of the small pamphlet stood an earthly model of nothing less than Swedenborg's Heaven itself. It had been there all along, waiting for me, beckoning to me from the City of Angels, calling me home.

The Getty Center.

Three hundred miles and less than a day later, friends, I was standing in line at the Getty Center's Lower Tram Station, surrounded by a host of fellow pilgrims. I had crossed a desert to get there, but many around me had come much further, risking perilous hardships, trekking across the country and even over the ocean to see what lay on the hilltop above us. Their voices, rushing in and out around me like the tide, trembled with excitement. A woman standing in front of me, wearing a faded Billy Ray Cyrus T-shirt, turned and surprisingly remarked, "I heard this is a lot better than that Bellagio in Las Vegas." I smiled. As she and I talked, a little tram pulled up to the terminal, and a man in a bright red coat directed us forward. He handed me a pamphlet, just like the one that had led me to the Getty, and smiled brightly as I passed into the comfortable interior of the little tram. As we began to move soundlessly forward, up the hillside, I looked at the people around me, feeling suddenly blissful.

The bright Southern California light washed across their faces, chasing away shadows and blemishes, smoothing wrinkles and flushing cheeks. I turned to the young woman sitting beside me, and gasped. The pollution level in Los Angeles that day seemingly had the effect on her face of those lovely films made in the nineteen forties and fifties, with their romantic close-ups and filters. As we moved up the hills, the edges of things slowly dissipated, turning the whole world around me into a lovely blur. I sighed, settled back into my seat, chuckling as I watched two little deer prance over the hillside to my right, and then, looking down at the pamphlet on my lap, laughed even louder as a quote by the Getty Center's architect Richard Meier caught my eye: "The tram ride is designed to give visitors a feeling of being elevated out of their day-to-day experience." He adds that, following their ascent, "visitors will have a powerful sense of being in the center of this great city." Oh, Richard, I thought, you do not even realize that you are just a tool . . . a tool in the Hand of God. At that moment, the little tram came to a gentle stop.

The Rapture was complete. As the doors opened, I bustled out onto the streets of Heaven.

† †

In the early Middle Ages, monasteries were often built in secluded, out-of-the-way places—in the middle of impenetrable forests, on mountain tops, or far from the city in uninhabited frontiers. There, away from temptation, monks could devote themselves to a life of contemplation. They followed St. Benedict's rule of *ora et labora*—pray and work. Their days were filled with back-breaking labor: tilling the soil, growing and harvesting crops, praying for sufficient rain, and fearing the threat of a bad harvest. They understood the hardships of a peasant's life and as such were particularly responsive to the biblical story of paradise as related in Genesis. As you well know, my lambs, the story recounts humanity's fall from a nobler state, how temptation led Adam and Eve away from their carefree life of pleasure and bounty and into a miserably laborious existence. The monks gladly accepted their fate as children of the expelled, but they knew in their hearts that eventually things would change. Someday, God would reverse the Fall, and restore Paradise on earth, where all the righteous would be released from their toils.

The Elucidation, a Bavarian monastic manual written around 1100 A.D., describes Heaven in great detail. After the Last Judgment, it reveals that God will remove all consequences of the Fall: "The punishment for sin, that is, coldness, heat, hail, and storm, will utterly disappear. The earth, in whose bosom the body of the Lord lay, will be like Paradise in its entirety and, because of having been irrigated with the blood of the saints, it will be decorated eternally with sweet-smelling flowers, lilies, roses, and violets that will never fade."

All of these things passed through my mind as I walked across the Getty Center's grand plaza built of travertine stone, up and down a series of steps, and into a luxuriant garden designed by artist Robert Irwin in an obvious state of divine grace. Down a zigzagging path, winding around a flowing stream, I slowly strolled, reveling in the plethora of flowers and plants lining the walkway: daylilies, California poppies, deer grass, irises and corkscrew rushes . . . the sheer numbers made my head swim. The path would occasionally cross over the water, and as I descended further, to my delight, I realized that the placement of the stones in the water at each of these junctures created very different sounds; one, deep and resonant, another, tinkling like a chorus of bells. As I crossed the last bridge, I watched the water plunge over a stone wall and down into a great circular bowl, splashing into a large reflecting pool. The pool entranced me, for there, in its center, twisted a maze of azaleas burning as red as the blood of Christ. The pattern of the maze created three interlocking circles, one of the earliest symbols of the Trinity. I longed to dive into that pure water and lose myself within that maze, surrendering to the complexity of the Three, but instead I turned away, content with the image burned in circles of fire on my heart, and looked up to the white towers looming above me . . . calling me into their embrace.

At the top of a steep staircase, I walked onto a long courtyard surrounded by tall buildings of stone, glass, and metal, sparkling brilliantly in the sunlight. To my right was a stone bench, and I sat down, looking deeply into a shallow pool that stretched out before my feet. I closed my eyes and wandered away from the gardens.

During the Renaissance, as civilization was transformed from a rural, agrarian model to become centered within cities, the representation of Heaven as portrayed in Revelation 21 began to take precedence in the minds of leading theologians. John, the author of Revelation, envisioned Heaven as no longer a garden but a majestic city built of jasper and gold, garnished with precious stones and gates of pearl, a place of unearthly light and beauty. As Christian thought embraced this newly accepted repertoire of urban imagery, the very liturgy of the church changed. "May the angels lead you to Paradise," sang the priests, "may the martyrs welcome you when you arrive, and may they guide you into the Holy City of Jerusalem." The text suggested that the soul would enter first a garden, and then the metropolis of Heaven.

In 1250 A.D., Gerardesca, a woman tertiary of the Camaldolese order, described the Holy City as filled with tall buildings wrought of crystal surrounded by long avenues paved in gold and precious stone, a place filled with pleasure gardens where the citizens of Heaven could run naked and free in tall luminescent grasses as bright as emeralds. Opening my eyes to the tall white palaces, stacked terraces, panes of curved glass, and gleaming steel, and looking across the courtyard to a 120-foot long fountain and a row of graceful cypress trees, I saw the Getty Center through Gerardesca's eyes. There, before me, I am sure that I also saw a number of lithe, beautiful bodies dancing across the square, their alabaster skin flashing in the radiance of divine countenance. I leapt to my feet, rubbing my eyes, and stumbled past the fountain and trees, hoping to catch another glimpse of the angelic streakers. Drunkenly, I pushed through a door, almost fell, and, looking up, found myself engulfed in a sea of flesh.

I had found the Heavenly Host.

Brothers and Sisters, for many hours I walked from room to room in the palaces of the Getty Center, and in its sacred halls I witnessed vision after vision of beautiful, naked bodies, so perfect, so divine, that they could only represent Bishop Augustine's supermodel version of

Heaven, as he describes it in his treatise *City of God* (413-27 A.D.): "Physical beauty will reign, and the eye will never be offended." It was the Bishop's belief that in Heaven "all bodily blemishes that mar human beauty will be removed," seemingly retouched by some angelic air-brush. Embarrassed, I found myself at times sucking in my ponderous stomach, longing for the day when I would step through the Pearly Gates and find myself sporting the washboard abs and golden locks of the glam-rock Adonis in Jacques-Louis David's *The Farewell of Telemachus and Eucharis* of 1818. I wanted to lay naked on a bed of flowers like some wilting princess as portrayed in Dosso Dossi's *Mythological Scene* of 1524, or frolic on a couch like the friends depicted in Gericault's *Three Lovers* of 1817. I longed to dive into the cold, dark waters of Thomas Eakins's 1883 *The Swimming Hole,* skinny-dipping like I never have before. I wanted to take the cow ride, as demonstrated in *The Abduction of Europa* of 1632 by Rembrandt, and then nap in the bed painted by Jaochim Wtewarl in his *Mars and Venus Surprised by Vulcan* of 1606.

Oh, beloved, to wear the red silk robes of Agostino Pallavicini, as captured in a 1621 portrait by Anthony van Dyck, while eating plate after plate of chicken and waffles on a bed like the one from 1760 attributed to Jacques-Jean-Baptiste Tilliard. Then, and only then, would I truly know that I had died and gone to Heaven! Oh, friends, time began to slip away as I wondered through darkened rooms filled with hundreds of illuminated manuscripts, each a human testament of love for the divine, medieval in their origin yet timeless in their devotion. I cannot express to you how my heart was ensnared by such endearing traps as the French *Book of Hours* of 1415 or the prayerbook of Charles the Bold of 1469. I cannot describe the fever that seemed to rob me of any knowledge of who I was, or where I was. I only slightly remember someone in a red coat telling me I was standing too close to Vincent van Gogh's *Irises* of 1889. I was dazed, confused, but filled with a lilting happiness that seemed to lift me from the floor and float me from sunlit room to sunlit room.

But then, my congregation, something stopped me dead in my tracks, and reality came flooding back, pounding into my skull like a sledgehammer. Before me hung a massive painting, all reds and greens, its surface thick and frothy with paint. It depicted a parade; its marchers, a crowd of leering psychotics and drugged-up band members, lumbered toward me. But to them, my friends, well, I paid little attention, for there, way back in the distance, riding on a little donkey, His head illuminated in gold, was my main man Jesus, waving to the crowds, waving to me. As I stared deeply into the painting, reveling in James Ensor's 1888 vision of *Christ's Entry into Brussels in 1889,* a voice inside my head began to chant, HE IS COMING! HE IS COMING! CHRIST IS COMING BACK! I knew it was true, I just knew it . . . but I also knew that I was wasting my time here. Ensor's painting had snapped me back to mundane existence, snatched the lie away from my slavering jaws like a well-worn chew toy, reminding me that the Rapture still hadn't occurred . . .

not yet, but soon. The Getty Center was not Heaven, only an earthly facsimile. I had spent the day in a *virtual* Heaven, certainly beautiful and enchanting, but unable to quench my burning spiritual thirst.

Since the time of this epiphany, my Brothers and Sisters, I have continued my peripatetic longings. But at the beginning of the new millennium, I returned to Las Vegas, and, to my dismay, discovered that the Rapture did not occur. To tell you that I'm not disappointed, even angry, would be a lie.

I float in an ocean of darkness, my children. And I think back to the middle of one particular afternoon—according to my wife, the Rev. Mrs., a bright and beautiful January eighth. The first January eighth of a whole new millennium. Bah! I remember feeling absolutely no interest. But I would like to relate to you a little story that brought truth to my tortured mind. In the cool, candlelit recesses of my Las Vegas apartment, its windows blocked out with aluminum foil, the sunlight is banned, turned away like an unfashionable dork from a chic Hollywood nightclub. I wanted no sunbeams here. I wanted no bill-collector eyes. No cable guy. No Mormons. I wanted nothing to disturb the depression sucking at my heart like a greedy infant on a ripe teat. I had no wants at all, beloved, because that thing I wanted most—the object of my ultimate desire—well, it was snatched away. I felt so unsatisfied. No explosions, no chaos . . . why, even Arnold Schwarzenegger knew that his film *End of Days* must conclude with a big bang. So, if Hollywood knows this, why doesn't GOD?! My friends, after visiting the Getty I just wanted to give up. I wanted to forget God. I wanted to forget Heaven. I just wanted to breathe in deeply the waters of my sorrow and drown in a Godless ocean. . . .

But, as I began to sink beneath the waves of despair, something caught my eye. Movement. A sleek, dark shadow down there at the end of the hallway, slinking toward me. A click, click, click of nails on linoleum, and the shape slithered ever closer to my chair, its movements slowing, slowing, as the distance between us fell away. The beast stood before me, in all its glory! Its breath was hot on my bare legs, and in its mouth hung limply what looked like the sloppy remains of some dead animal. The head of the creature lowered, so gently, and with a wet plop, the "dead thing" fell to the floor. But this was no grisly carcass, my darlings, no . . . it was Binky, an overly loved stuffed toy, and the beast was none other than my dog Achilles, a ridiculous twit of a Black Lab.

Achilles made an impatient snorting sound, and I noticed, as I focused hard on the two brown eyes hovering there above my knees, that he was desperately harnessing all his doggy psychokinetic power. Over and over, he stared into my eyes, and then slowly looked down between my feet at the wet mess that once was a stuffed rabbit. In prior lives, my dog's companion had been a bear, a bug, a tiger, a Bart Simpson, and a radish, always given, due to Achilles's limited vocabulary, the same name. We are on the 15th incarnation of Binky, and at the moment he just lay there . . . waiting, staring up at me with one chewed button-eye, well aware of what comes next, well aware of the GAME. I sigh. It seemed that between the sunny observations of my optimistic wife and the oral fixation of my silly dog, I had no choice but to get back into my routine, regardless of my heartache, regardless of my longing.

I reached down slowly between my knees toward the stuffed animal resting beside my left foot. Achilles suddenly grew tense, and even in the darkness I could see the hair at the base of his neck standing up. His breathing slowed, and his ears perked up as my hand got closer to the matted ball of fake fur. Six inches and it would be mine. Five. Four inches. Three. With a growl, Achilles leapt forward, snatching the toy away from my hand. He threw his muzzle back, shaking his head back and forth, his whole squirming body turning in a complete circle, and then he ran clumsily back down the hallway, his wagging tail knocking over a small table laden with candles. The candles, their flames dancing as they fall, landed in the deep brown carpeting. Whoosh!!! Flames leapt up from the carpet, bathing the room in a hellish light. Well, beloved, I just sat there for a few moments, mesmerized by the flames hungrily spreading across the floor. Then, with a very unmanly scream, I leapt to my feet and rushed toward the kitchen to get the small extinguisher mounted beside the stove. I flew back into the living room, tearing away the pin, and pulled the lever. A fine white spray hit me in the face, its taste something akin to stale menthol. Cursing, I turned the extinguisher's nozzle away from me and toward the flames. There was a moment when it seemed that the white foam would be no match for the fire, but, as quickly as it was given birth to, the fire died, and was no more.

Coughing, I walked over to the window and wrenched it open. Sunlight spilled into the room, chasing away the shadows and turning the motes of dust and ash hanging in the air into twinkling, swirling little galaxies that danced away in the afternoon breeze. As I stood there, Achilles walked nonchalantly out of the hallway, across the ruined carpet, until he stood directly before me. He dropped his Binky at my feet, and then stepped back, his gaze wandering from the sloppy little toy, up to my eyes, and then back again to his treasure. He waited impatiently.

I began to laugh, and as I did, beloved, my spirit soared. I found Rapture, I found understanding, and I found God—but not up there in the sky, no. I found Him in the obsessed eyes of a crazy dog. At the time, I realized that the Getty Center is none other than one of God's latest toys, my friends. Dropped at our feet, it sits there, tempting us with a brief glimpse through the divine curtain into the maker's boudoir. It is a testament to humanity's faith in the presence of God and His Heavenly Kingdom. Its very existence is proof that the Game will continue: humankind, blindly reaching for a little taste of perfect knowledge, and God, snatching it away at the very last moment, laughing as He runs into the darkness. You know, my wife was right, it was a beautiful day in post-millenial America. Now, don't get me wrong, some Arnold-esque explosions would have been nice. But, at the time, as I looked out my window and into a glorious Nevada sunset, I was pretty satisfied with the promise of something even better, even more Hollywood, than a great flaming finale. I thought back to the Getty, and to what man has wrought, and is capable of building in the future. I'm talking *sequel,* baby!

The Exorcism of the Santa Monica Museum of Art

|a performance on Good Friday, April 13, 2001|

I EXORCISE THEE, every unclean spirit, in the name of God, the Father Almighty, and in the name of Jesus Christ, His Son, our Lord and Judge, and in the power of the Holy Spirit, that thou depart from this house, the Santa Monica Museum of Art, created to be a holy temple of creation, that it may be made a temple of the living God and that the Holy Spirit may dwell therein. Through the name of Christ our Lord, who shall come to judge the living and the dead, and the world by fire:

Olive Branches

Hail, God of Abraham!
Hail, God of Isaac!
Hail, God of Jacob!
Jesus the Righteous
Son of the Father
    Below the seven
    Within the seven
Come Yao Saboath!!!!

Direct your power to the Santa Monica Museum of Art. Drive Satan, this unclean demon within this Hall, away!! I command you, Demon, whoever you may be, by the power of God eternal . . .

Sabarbarbathioth
Sabarbarbathiouth
Sabarbarbathioneth
Sabarbarbaphai

Come out Demon, whoever you may be.
Stay away from the Santa Monica Museum of Art.
Quickly! Now! Come Out Demon!
I bind you with unbreakable chains of adamantine!
I cast you into the Abyss of Hell!!!!!!

Spittle from Mouth

Be Opened, oh Temple of God, and to you, O Devil, BEGONE, for the judgment of God is at hand!!!!

Holy Water

I consecrate you with the water of the River Jordan, in the name of the Father, the Son, and the Holy Spirit.

Chrism of Salvation

May Almighty God the Father, who has regenerated you with water and the Holy Spirit, and given thee remission of all thy sins, anoint thee with the chrism of salvation, in the name of Christ our Lord, unto Life everlasting.

Oil of Salvation

I anoint thee with the oil of salvation in the name of Christ, that thou mayest have life everlasting.

And now, oh Great Hall, receive this light, as a symbol of the fire that will burn at the roots of your foundation. A light of truth and understanding, a light of hope, a Holy light to illuminate the hearts of each and every soul who passes through your mighty doors, seeking answers to all questions human.

God blesses you, Santa Monica Museum of Art!

Exercising Demons

HALLELUJAH, my Brothers and Sisters. I am so glad, so proud that you have all come to commune with me today, here in God's sublime wilderness. For on this day we are most certainly kinsmen, if not by blood, then at least bound together by a common dream. And what do we dream for? Wealth? (There is a resounding "NO!!!" from the audience.) Love? (Again, another loud "NO!") Do we, Men and Women of Dreams, long for power? ("NOOOO!!!!" the people scream.) Oh, I know the desire that curdles in your hearts. I know it, for it is a dream that I too have had for some time. It is our heart's desire, locked deep down inside our souls where our girlfriends, our boyfriends, and our spouses can never find it. I'm telling you, when we're all there on our knees in the dark, each looking up at our inspirational picture of Brad Pitt on the wall, surrounded by our Ab-Rollers, our Nordic Tracks, and our Thigh Masters, we are certain that if this one wish were granted by God, then the fulfillment of all those other desires—for wealth, power, and love—will just follow along like baby ducks chasing their mama. And what, pray tell, is that dream? Come on, all of you, on your knees, and let's say it together. Hurry up, now! Good. Repeat after me: "OH LORD, THOU WHO ART ABOVE ALL THINGS, O GREAT SPINNER OF THE COSMIC THREAD, BINDER OF THE MORTAL COIL, HEAR OUR PRAYER! GRANT

THIS THAT WE WISH FOR ABOVE ALL THINGS, OH FATHER. MAKE US THIN! MAKE US THIN! MAKE US THIN!"

Well, you are lost, my little lambs. Lost, bleating sorrowfully out there in the darkness. I can hear the sorrow in your voices. I can see the doubt in your wet, doelike eyes. Trust me when I say that I too have shared the feelings locked away in your hearts. I have tasted your tears on my own lips, for they have sprung from my own eyes. I too have wanted to be thin. Oh, to be able to buy leather pants. To be able to sit comfortably in an airplane seat. Blessed God, if that kid working at McDonald's just for once wouldn't automatically super-size my Big Mac Combo, I probably would jump across the counter and give her a big, ol' sloppy kiss! But, my Brothers and Sisters, are we willing to sell our souls just to be thin? No, I believe we are damning ourselves for a much more lofty goal than a size 30 waist. I know, for I almost sold out. I almost fell into the pit dug by the Devil. But I escaped. And so can you. Put away your tom-toms and your war paint, muffle your cries and listen to me. Today, I'm going to give you the keys, not to thindom, but to pass into the Kingdom. I'm going to show you the way back to Paradise, and all you have to do is listen to this, my testimony.

My name is Ethan. I am 30 years old and weigh 228 pounds, and I want to be an angel. I thought I wanted to be thin, but that was a silly dream concocted by watching too much *Baywatch* and MTV. No, I want to be an angel. Hell, I guess I always wanted to be one. Trust me, this isn't some spur-of-the-moment idea. No sirree, Bob, I've thought about this for a long time, and I really believe it is what God wants for me, too. You see, my Brothers and Sisters, I've been hearing voices lately. Sugary voices coming at me from the media, the artworld, my friends and family. Surely, only God can speak through them, right? I mean, they *sound* so sincere. My mother: "Ethan, wearing all black doesn't necessarily make you look thin!" My best friend Beady: "They say that when you hit 30, Ethan, you really begin to spread out!" An art critic introducing me to a museum board: "The Reverend is a wonderful example of a little-known evolutionary principle, Survival of the Fattest!"

I suppose all these barbed comments were supposed to make me a better man, a better minister, and a better artist. They do call it "tough love," for Heaven's sake. I should have learned this lesson from Richard Simmons on late-night television, but alas, I had to be spanked and made to stand in a corner many times before I truly understood. Eventually, I figured it out, but not under the guidance of my friends, my gallery dealer, or Suzanne Sommers. No, I always believed that each of them simply wanted me to have looser pants. I couldn't imagine that God—through them—wanted me to be a member of the Heavenly Host. Or so I came to believe. But it was a lie, a false epiphany that would come from the most unlikely of sources . . . the famous actor, Mr. Brad Pitt.

I was in the "10 Items or Less" line of an Albertson's Grocery Store. As I waited, I did what I always do, and patiently looked through the tabloids. The cover of one caught my eye. I picked it up. There, in glorious color, was a still taken from the film *Fight Club,* showing a shirtless Brad Pitt standing in a basement, surrounded by a number of angry-looking men. As I looked at Brad's rippling abdominal muscles, a statement made by my lovely wife Lisa the night before floated into my mind, on wings of gossamer. We had been watching *Seven Years in Tibet* on cable, when she exclaimed, "My God, look at him! He is soooo fine! He's an angel!" An angel. My sweet Lisa, the person more dear to me than anyone else in this life, thought Brad Pitt an angel. Now, beloved, even as a minister, I haven't thought a lot about angels. I mean, I've always considered them the good Lord's custodians, nothing more. But as I stood there in that supermarket, the hungry expletives of my wife buzzing around in my skull like bees in a hive, I had a moment of clarity. There's a mathematical postulate which states that if *a* equals *b,* and *b* equals *c,* then *a* must equal *c.* My Brothers and Sisters, without a doubt, I wanted to *be* Brad Pitt; and, I wager, a majority will concur that Brad Pitt is an angel. So therefore I, Rev. Ethan Acres, must want to be an angel.

How did I go about becoming an angel? The first clue wasn't very hard to find. For, as I replaced the tabloid, I noticed that the rack directly below was filled with copies of a small red, white, and yellow book entitled *A Week in the Zone* by Barry Sears, Ph.D. Its bright, cheerful cover beckoned me to "join the Low-Carb Revolution!" Barry promised that if I truly dedicated myself to his teachings, my life would change forever. Oh, beloved, as if the word of a genuine Ph.D. wasn't enough, I had simply to look at the back cover of the book to have all my doubts burned away like so much early-morning dew. Emblazoned in chartreuse letters was a quote from *Woman's World* magazine: "The Zone Is the Hottest Diet in Hollywood!" That's all I needed to know. I snatched up the little book and abandoned my grocery cart filled with Ben and Jerry's Ice Cream, Dorito's, and slices of individually wrapped Kraft American cheese. An ATM card-swipe later, I was bustling ecstatically out into a bright, lowfat world.

In the days that followed, I wandered into the Zone. Truly, Brethren, Dr. Sears was a fount of inspiration that seemed never to run dry. But even with his warm anecdotes and catchy soundbites, I felt I needed more. I mean, gosh, *my* endeavor was much greater than mere dieting: I was on a higher path. I was becoming a better person, an angelic being. I was fasting. I began to read everything I could find on the subject. This is how I saw it. We men of God have been obsessed with dietary concerns for a long time. Fasting—the renunciation of food for the purpose of spiritual growth—has always been a cornerstone of Christian piety, not just a feat of endurance and discipline distinguishing the elite and heroic few, but a powerful tool for regimenting the day-to-day existence of the serious ascetic. Let me enlighten you, my Brothers and Sisters, with a few lines from a fourth-century Greek treatise on virginity: "Observe what fasting does. It dries up the bodily humors, casts out demons, and chases away evil thoughts; it sanctifies the body and places the person before the throne of God . . . For fasting is the life of the angels, and the one who makes use of it has angelic rank."

In fact, many Christian theologians believe that the only way back to Paradise is to become more angelic of body, thereby reversing The Fall and restoring virgin purity to Creation.

That's right, you heard me, my Brothers and Sisters . . . my goal was virgin purity. You see, according to early Christian writers, there is no room in Paradise for sex. The Cappadocian writer Gregory of Nyssa (ca. 335-394) believed that once Adam and Eve were clothed by God in "tunics of skins" (Genesis 3:21), they "assumed the passable and passionate, coporeal-sexual condition" that continues to mark humanity's fall. Gregory would go on to propose that skin tunics are simply "forms of the irrational animal nature with which we were clothed because of our familiarity with the passionate life: sexual intercourse, conception, childbirth, uncleanness, nursing, feeding, excretion, old age, and death." Therefore, in order to become like angels—"perfect, rational, noncorporeal beings of air and light, devoid of earthly passions"—we must rid ourselves of our tunics of skin. In other words, beloved, our bodies must go, with all their lusty flaws. And what is the best way to get rid of unsightly pounds? Well, fasting. And, oh, lest I forget, please take note of one other thing that these great minds are quick to point out. Fasting serves not only to make you look like an angel—all thin, pale, and light on your feet—it also makes you *act* like an angel, no longer troubled by the needs of your earthly vessel.

By now, I'm sure you're squirming away there in your seats, saying "Hey, I never said I wanted to be an angel; what does this have to do with me?" But, my point is that you don't *have* to say it. The desire to be an angel is so tangled up with the foundations of Western culture that you can't throw a stone without hitting some example of Angelology. (For Heaven's Sake, many of you here today have made Los Angeles, the City of Angels, your home.) You, my Brothers and Sisters, are being subliminally bombarded everyday with angelic signals that are moving you toward your halo-sporting, tutu-wearing, wing-flapping destinies. Look, let's say you spend an evening at some fancy-pants art gallery, then go grab a bite at some Frenchy little restaurant, and finish out the night on your cushy sofas watching television. Well, hell, beloved, get out your harps and play me a little ditty, because you could very well be a member of the choir already! Yes, you heard me, repent, for the signs are at hand.

The next time you find yourself shuffling solemnly around one of your favorite galleries, look closely at some of the paintings hanging there on the walls. Aren't they pretty? They are so bright and cheerful. The thinly layered paint flowing across their polished surfaces always reminds me of flesh. Beautiful flesh. Sometimes, when the art dealer isn't around, I even reach out and touch them . . . delicately, lovingly, fearfully. Standing in art galleries always reminds me of going to funeral parlors. Both are big, white rooms filled with people dressed in black, congregating together to see the body of their loved one and remarking in hushed whispers about how good the dearly departed looks . . . how lifelike. Looking at paintings, I always remember the faces of those sweet dead, also painted bright and cheerful, completely at peace. I used to wonder, why? But now I understand.

For centuries, writers have compared the structure of the human body to that of a painting. In fact, it began not long after the first paintings rendered on linen (admired for their portability and resistance to moisture) left the Netherlands for Italy in the fifteenth century. Paintings very much like Dieric Bouts's *Annunciation* (which you may view for yourself at the Getty Museum, on a hilltop above the City of Angels) would greatly influence artists such as the great Italian Giovanni Bellini, and forever change the way paintings were executed. Giorgio Vasari, in his 1568 *Lives of Painters,* was one of the first to look at pigment mixed with glue (made from animal skin), canvas, and stretcher bars as an allegory for the human body's skin, musculature, and skeletal framework.

This idea would continue to haunt the imaginations of artists for generations. Mark Rothko, that twentieth-century painter of luminous abstractions, anthropomorphized his paintings, even referring to them as living presences. One statement by Rothko stands out above all others: "Paintings are skins that are shed and hung on a wall." Have we not already spoken today of shedding our tunics of skin, in order to return to Paradise? It's no wonder that galleries and funeral parlors appear to be so similar. We go to each for reassurance. Both glorious paintings on the wall and dead bodies in their boxes show us that in order to pass on—and become angels—we must let go of our earthly forms. In fact, the process of becoming angelic is a process of becoming Christlike. As

Christians, beloved, the very symbol of our faith, the crucifix, represents the savior's flesh stretched across bars of wood, hung on a wall. As such, all paintings remind us of Christ and what we must give up in order to become His angels.

After going to an art gallery, Friends, we always feel painfully famished. Why not treat ourselves to a nice restaurant? They're everywhere, tasteful little bistros longing to take us under their eaves and give us a good old gastronomic pampering. But, if you haven't been out in a while, let me assure you that the face of fine dining has changed. Thankfully, its higher purpose is still intact. What higher purpose? Well, to turn us into angels, of course! Aren't you listening? The most popular trend today, "fusion cooking"—a blend of ethnic foods and ingredients into Western cuisine—owes much to the tradition of "nouvelle cuisine" that arose in the nineteen seventies and eighties. Such cuisine and high-priced progeny are characterized by bite-size portions artistically arranged and dribbled with light sauces. My Brothers and Sisters, we must applaud the wondrous chefs who created this style of cooking, not for the magic they have spawned in kitchens across this great nation of ours, but for their tireless effort to create a place where we can go to achieve so many of the goals of Angeldom: There, amid sparkling crystal flowers (often with abstract "shed skin" paintings hanging on their walls), we may starve away our bodies, climbing another step toward Heaven's Gate. Halleluiah!

When you get home, brethren, turn on your televisions. I suggest flipping the dial over to CBS, the Tiffany

Network, where you might see *Touched by an Angel,* or, better yet, one of the new shows of reality programming. *Survivor* allows the television audience to look on as a small group of people is coerced into living a regimented, monastic life with the hope of achieving some final reward at the end of the season. "Forced asceticism" plays a central role, as the "castaways" spend thirty-nine days eating rats, bugs, and whatever bottom-feeding sea life they can spear. They commune together every third day at a tribal meeting, where the group must vote one of their own off the island. *Every third day.* Sound familiar? Of course, it does. "On the third day, Christ rose from the dead." (The Apostle's Creed)

Survivor proposes as its model nothing less than a collective decision-making process that regularly names one of its members "worthy" of passing into oblivion . . . into Glory. Look carefully at who leaves and who stays, who passes on and who remains behind to continue bettering themselves. In its first season, it cannot surprise us that Dirk, the 23-year-old Bible-thumping Wisconsonite, and Sonya, the 63-year-old Californian singing "cum-ba-yah" while strumming away on her ukulele, "die" very early, whereas Richard, the 39-year-old, overweight, gay corporate trainer from Rhode Island must stay until the very end. Richard *can't* leave, not because he's shrewd and plays the game well. He must stay on the island until the collective mind deems him worthy to ascend from hell and take his place in the Heavenly Chorus. He must drop a few pounds and stop prancing about naked, making passes at cute guys. If Richard refuses to give up the world, *Survivor* proposes that he cannot be an angel, and in fact must take a million dollars in order to seal his worldly fate . . . possibly damning him to hell.

So, beloved, face the facts. You are being pushed from all sides, corralled into becoming good little angels. It's wonderful to be on this path of happiness and joy, right? Wrong. For beloved, I have walked this path and found no joy. I have found only bitterness and despair. I told you that to become an angel, I wandered into the wilderness of a deep fast. For two weeks, I became the disciple of Gregory and Basil and Evagrius. My daily caloric intake fell to an average of 1,200. My meals ranged from yummy lunches consisting of three whole ounces of chicken breast and a slice of apple to dinner plates overflowing with sometimes as much as five ounces of salmon with a cup of mixed berries on the side. As I wolfed down that salmon and berries and those egg-white omelets, I did lose weight, oh yes, indeed . . . but I also began to lose something else.

It is well documented that drastic dieting not only causes weight loss but also may result in emaciation (the wasting of muscle), edema (the retention of fluids in body tissue), hair loss, increased tolerance to heat, decreased tolerance to cold, lowered pulse rate, lowered basal metabolism, as well as increases in depression, apathy, tiredness, weakness, and irritability. Most important for our message today, beloved, is that prolonged fasting results in a marked weakening or loss of sexual desire and activity . . . a lost sex drive that is often found not to return even after the resumption of normal dietary habits. In the Zone, I began to fall apart, both physically and mentally. Of course, I didn't really mind when some of the hair on my back fell out, but one evening, when my wife asked me to join her for one of our ritualistic jaunts in the shower, I was appalled to hear myself say, "I want to finish watching the Republican Convention."

I now know that the true force behind those whispering voices come from none other than Old Horny himself. Friends, I promised that I would show you the way to the Kingdom. Well, let me tell you, the path to Paradise does not lie through the Valley of the Zone. Lost in that bitter wasteland, I came to see it not as a promised utopia but as a suburb of hell. As a castaway in that nightmarish realm, I served not the will of God but the Dark Master. I made my life a regimented Inferno, alienating myself from my friends, wife, and son. This is the diabolical perfection of the Devil's plan. You see, Satan's sole purpose is to keep us from finding the path to the Kingdom. His very name, the Devil, is translated from the Greek *diablos* and means "an obstacle in one's path."

The ascetic can most certainly use fasting to focus his or her mind on the Creator. And God Bless Barry Sears, there is nothing wrong with the Zone Diet. But I believe that the Devil himself is using these constructions of humanity to dig a great pit in our path, a Brad Pitt, an unrealistic image that we have been tricked to believe will make us better, stronger, more angelic of body and soul. My Brethren, this is a pipe dream that we can never achieve. I tried. But did I find myself becoming an angel? No. I came to know only anger and despair. No matter how much weight I lost, it was never enough. I would look at myself in the mirror and see a soul burning in the sinful fires of gluttony.

Did you know that Christ himself was accused of being a glutton? In Matthew 11, the Pharisees said of Christ, "Behold a man gluttonous, and a winebibber, a friend of publicans and sinners." Friends, it is not a sin to love food and drink. In fact, it is Christlike. It is only sinful when we become so obsessed with food that we forget how to live. In the prison of my deep fast, my obsession with food only increased. In fact, as I constantly weighed myself and prepared my balanced little meals, food became the center of my life. *I stopped living.* And this, my Friends, is the ultimate blasphemy, the ultimate sin: an abomination that can bar the way back to The Garden forever.

For, my Brothers and Sisters, the only way back to Paradise is through accepting ourselves as we are, not by starving ourselves into a shape we call angelic. God created us in His image. (Genesis 1:27) For this reason, my Brothers and Sisters, we should look toward our love handles and see them not as evil, but Holy. Oh Warriors of Creation, we should wear our "tunics of skin" as armor. We should not shy away from hearty meals, creative television, passionate sex, and paintings depicting all sorts of earthly delights. The Devil will continue to lash out at us, wrapped in the guise of such exercising demons as Billy Blank and Jane Fonda. Like Jacob in Genesis 32, we must tear at his designer wings, gouge out his baby blue eyes, loosen his perfectly straight bridgework. In that bone-crushing mêlée, we may forget about becoming angels and embrace the gift of our humanity. Then, we may bite ravenously from the sweet fruit of life, filling our spiritual bellies with arts both fine and popular, and be exiles no more. We may leave that arena as the Creator's Heavyweight Champions. And He will be there, waiting to wrap His treelike arms around us, His prodigal sons. He will kiss our cheeks. He will welcome us home. We will know the blessing of God.

Dear Jerry

[a performance at the University of Southern Mississippi on September 14, 2000 and Mississippi Gulf Coast Community College on September 18, 2000]

IN MARCH 1999, The Reverend Jerry Falwell denounced the Teletubbie Tinky Winky, criticizing the television personality's choice of lifestyle as "unsuitable for children." Mr. Winky, a private soul living just outside London, never issued a public response. Until now . . .

Dear Jerry,

I saw you the other day on the tele. You looked so fine in your dark suit and striped tie. You were poetry in motion, Jerry. It doesn't matter that you've gained a few pounds. (Me too.) I don't care that your vision isn't what it used to be. In fact, when I see you standing on stage, dear heart, in front of all those people, I get a thrill just watching the spotlights sparkling like fireworks on the rims of your glasses. I adore you.

So, you must understand why I'm feeling so much pain today. Why do you torture me so, Jerry? Sometimes, the words that fall from your lips cut me like knives. I hear you on the radio or see you on Larry King, and I just die, Jerry. I just die. After all these years . . . well, I really thought that I had come to know you. I *believed* in you. It's true, rarely have I agreed with your politics, but whenever I look at you I see a man who is willing to face the big issues with the courage of a lion. And you are a lion,

Jerry . . . you are "a-lion" about me all over town! A threat to children? *Please.* I have tears in my eyes. You shouldn't go around throwing stones. We all live in glass houses, sweetie.

Jerry, we really aren't all that different. We both reach out to millions of people each day. We both use all the good Lord gave us to make the world a better place. And we both want to bring a little light into the lives of those we care about.

But I guess you see only the differences. You like to wear beautifully tailored suits. Well, Jerry, I too admire a nice frock as much as the next guy. But let's get real. Teletubbieland is *so* warm and humid. A nice suit like yours would last about as long here as a snowball in hell (if you'll forgive me the expression). And, oh, what a shame that would be! Me? I just like to hang out naked. For Heaven's sake, the man upstairs gave me this fabulous skin of purple velour, and, sister, I don't think he'd appreciate me covering up a miracle as fine as this one.

In your back pocket, Jerry, I'm sure you carry a wallet of the softest lambskin. But look at me. Do you see any pockets? Hello. I have no choice but to carry a purse. C'mon, you know you can carry lots of things in a purse that would never fit in some cramped little wallet. Gumdrops and licorice fit very nicely there, Jerry. And so does a Bible. But would you guess what my most favorite thing in the whole wide world is to carry in my purse . . . *glitter!*

So, Jerry, I don't see why you hate me. It can't be because of my purses, or purple skin, or the triangle on my head. I mean, the Holy Trinity is represented by a triangle, isn't it? I guess I'll be patient with you. I learned that in Vacation Bible School. I also learned how to forgive. And I forgive you, my sweet Jerry.

I will keep hoping that one day, you and I may spend an afternoon together. I think you'll see then that I am not such a bad chap, after all. We will picnic in the most beautiful glen in all of Teletubbieland, munching on Tubbie toast dipped in Tubbie custard. We'll run barefoot and naked through the tall dewy grass, chasing bunnies and squirrels. I know, all the way down in my little Tubbie soul, that when that day comes, our hearts, for so long imprisoned like beautiful doves, will break free from their worldly cages. They will fly up into that great blue sky, and we will lose ourselves forever in the majestic splendor of Paradise, joined in perfect brotherly love.

Together at last, I will be able to whisper in your ear what we've suspected all along: "Jerry, you complete me."

XXXOOO,
Tinky Winky

Performance Anxiety

MY DARLING, I am writing to you as I look through the window of my room and out into the parking lot of the Apache Tears Motel, just off I-40 somewhere in the middle of New Mexico and not far from a little smudge on the map called Clines Corners. It is starting to get dark outside, and it probably would be easier to write if I turned on the frilly poodle-skirt lamp perched beside me atop a table made from a wagon wheel, but I don't want to. You see, lover, I don't want the lamplight to chase away the view through my little window. Just outside, a van is parked, a 1973 Ford Panel Wagon. It is a rather ordinary piece of American engineering, but, my darling, trust me when I tell you that there is something special about this particular brick on wheels. On its right flank, facing me now and gloriously illuminated by the setting sun, is an airbrushed mural depicting the story of Jael. (Judges 4:18-22) Do you remember this biblical scene? The Israelites were at war with the Canaanites. The commander of the Canaanite army was Sisera, who, having been defeated on the battlefield by the Prophetess Deborah, tried to hide in the tent of the Sorceress Jael. He would never know his folly, for, as soon as he fell asleep, Jael drove a tent stake through his head, nailing him to the ground, dead.

My darling, I really wish you could see this painting. You would be utterly shocked, not at the graphic nature of the story, nor at the liberties the artist took with the subject (Jael dressed all in black leather; Sisera bearing a striking resemblance to Kurt Cobain; and the murder weapon—not a tent stake, but a red, white, and blue Fender Stratocaster). Rather, I think, you would be shocked at how much you look like the painted Jael. Especially the eyes. Ice blue. Steely. Contemplative. You don't need a tent stake or a Fender Stratocaster, my beautiful temptress. Your eyes pierce through my skull just fine, thank you very much. Case in point: last night . . .

I guess you knew I had been watching you for some time. Reclining on the bed, I had merely to turn my head slightly to the left in order to peer into the bathroom where you were enjoying your nightly constitutional. Lying in the tub, surrounded by candles, your golden hair pulled up and restrained by a gingerly placed No. 2 Ticonderoga pencil, you were a perfect vision of loveliness. The candlelight made your skin glow like brightly polished alabaster, and the bubblebath created a rich froth that enveloped you like a delicate, sparkly cloud. As I approached the door leading into your fortress of solitude, I noticed that you were deeply absorbed in a bulky, leather-bound tome. I couldn't recognize the book, nor did I care to, so enraptured was I by the pout on your lips and the coltish perfection of your legs. I wanted to drop to my knees and recite to you the poetic strains from the seventh chapter of the "Song of Solomon": "The joints of thy thighs are like jewels, the work of thy hands cunning and true. Thy navel is like a round goblet, which wanteth not liquor: thy belly is like a heap of wheat set about with lilies. Thy breasts are like two young roes loose in the field!" But instead, my darling, the scripture failed me, and all I could ask, as you may well remember, was "What'cha reading?"

"Lippincott's Drug Guide for Nurses," you curtly answered.

"Uuummmmm . . . sounds sexy!" said I.

"Not really sexy, but . . . informative." Still pondering the book, you asked, "Ethan, how do you like the sound of clozapine?"

I shrugged my shoulders. "I don't know . . . what's it for?"

Then, my dear, the moment of truth came. You turned those hypnotic eyes toward me, burning through the front of my head like lasers, and said. "Well, baby, it's what they call an antipsychotic, and considering how freaky you've been acting lately, I think it's probably the perfect thing to fix you up!"

So, you think I'm mad. You are considering the possibility that I should be medicated. My dear, this revelation stings, but I'd be lying if I said that I haven't seen it coming. I've heard similar comments from others, you know. That panel I was on a few weeks ago, for instance. Did I tell you about it? Well, this famous artist actually said, right in front of the whole room, that every time I opened my mouth it made him break out in a rash, and that if I ever came to his house, he wouldn't hesitate to turn his hose on me. If comments from strangers weren't enough, pay special attention to the pamphlets my mother has been sending me lately about these wonderful therapeutic camps she thinks I should check out. Her words: "I just don't want to see you end up like your Uncle Dutch!" Have I ever told you about Uncle Dutch or his current project? He's building a UFO landing site somewhere deep in the Smokey Mountains of Gatlinburg, Tennessee.

Okay, okay. Granted, I'm not your average Joe. I like to dance around in angel wings and big diapers. I enjoy the sensation of pastries being hurled at my head, and, regardless of my ponderous belly, I think I look pretty fly in silver Spandex or purple body paint. And, yes, I regularly speak in public about my belief in God and my love for Christ, regardless of the fact that my listeners often run screaming for a bottle of Caladryl. I am a minister. I am also a performance artist. In both capacities, I serve the same purpose: catharsis.

Of course, I am in no way the first. Throughout history, from ancient religious rituals to the stages of vaudeville and the dark lounges of Las Vegas, culminating in the galleries and alternative spaces of contemporary art, men and women have used ritualized action to purge the collective mind, to bring the outside in, and to revitalize the fires of empathy in the human heart. Come, my one and only, take my metaphysical hand, and stroll with me down memory lane.

Imagine that you stand in a marketplace. You are in the city of Damascus, and it is the year 435 A.D. The city is a bustling center, and an ocean of people flows around you. Your eyes begin to water, dazzled by a light of that unearthly variety found only in the Mediterranean, and you feel feverishly excited about exploring the maze of booths and fruit stands scattered pell mell around you. But, my darling, you have only long enough to inhale a single breath of hot desert air before a piercing cry stops all those around you in their tracks. Following their collective gaze, you see the masses parting not far from where you stand, allowing the unimpeded passage of a solitary figure. He is dressed in rags stained with blood and feces. As he walks stiff-legged across the cobbled streets, you notice that tied to him, being dragged slowly along behind, is a dead dog. Angry yells begin to be heard, and stones fly through the air, but the figure continues to walk, ignoring the wrath of the mob.

He is Simeon, my dear . . . someday he will be known as St. Simeon, and he is a "Fool for Christ's Sake," a phrase coined by Paul of Tarsus in his letter to the Corinthians (1 Corinthians 4:10) and alluded to earlier in the accusing words of the Judaian prophet Hosea (Hosea 9:7). Now known as the Patron of Shepherds, Simeon is one of a number of men and women of God—"Fools for Christ"—who took the words of Paul to heart and chose a separate path from the orthodox to find their way to spiritual enlightenment. Not that they were rebelling against the Church (at least not yet!). In fact, the practice of Christianity was already beginning to lock down a specific set of rituals, all designed for one purpose: to allegorize the presence of the spiritual in the physical world, in order to give the unknowable a tangible existence. Consider the example of Baptism and its ritualized washing away of sin with water. The sacrament is an allegory of the internal process by means of which a human being washes away all the actions of bitterness and anger from his or her past and is reborn a spiritual infant, crawling forward into a new and exciting future.

The "fools" understood this emphatically. Yet, the stylized, highly ordered execution of the Church's rituals seemed to them a far cry from the self-effacement and self-negation prescribed by Paul, Hosea, and the very life of Christ (himself accused of madness and demonic possession). Therefore, the "fools" went their own way. Our boy Simeon would run naked into churches during Mass, extinguishing all the candles and screaming as he threw peanuts at the women. He spent the last thirty-five years of his life erecting and living atop sixty-foot pillars, screaming the word of God from on high. Likewise, in the sixth century, as John of Ephesus tells us, a wealthy couple named Theophilius and Maria gave all their possessions to the poor and wandered the countryside in the guise of a comedian and a prostitute. The two would demonstrate theatrically a wide variety of sexual acts in the streets, drawing great attention from onlookers, and then, at the climax (please excuse me!) of their performance, would stand together and break into religious song, preaching about the love of Christ.

In the thirteenth century, a respected notary, Jacopone da Todi, following the death of his beloved wife, would strip naked and crawl through the streets of Todi, wearing a saddle strapped to his back, naying like a horse, and inviting shocked onlookers to mount him for a ride to find Jesus. Mark the Mad, the naked Saint Basil the Blessed, Saint Sabas sitting atop piles of dung and eating beetles—

the list goes on. Yes, my dear, this blessed era of enlightenment lasted until the seventeenth century, when, with the dawning of the Age of Reason, saints and mystics were no longer tolerated. They were beaten, raped, and executed. French historian Michel Foucault called this period, with its overflowing asylums and penitentiaries, "The Great Confinement," and the economically troubled Europe of the time would lay the foundation for a spiritual impoverishment that would last for hundreds of years. That is, until vaudeville, when this same religious fervor found a new, unexpected home.

American vaudeville, my love, reached its full maturity by the year 1915. Its very name was derived from a series of songs written by a Norman miller named Oliver Basselin, in the fifteenth century. He called them *Vaux-de-Vire,* meaning drinking songs. The name would be corrupted to *voix de ville,* or "sounds of the town," and after about two hundred years would evolve into the French *vaudeville,* meaning a ballad or light form of comedy. As entertainment, the American form of vaudeville had its origins in British minstrel shows and music halls of the eighteen hundreds, but, in their desire to remain independent of Great Britain, the Americans adopted the French name. On the surface, you might see vaudeville as simply a theater for the masses—a plethora of variety acts, including songs, dances, acrobatic feats, skits, burlesque, and trained animals. But, my darling, it was so much more.

By the early twentieth century, America was in a completely traumatized state: The affliction was called Urbanization. Masses of European immigrants and rural

Americans were moving into the cities, looking for work and to better their lives. Once there, unable to retain contact with the folk art and rituals of their pasts, these new peoples looked around at their culturally impoverished surroundings and felt psychically destitute. The crowded and machine-ridden world that incredulous immigrants first met in New York, Chicago, Cincinnati, or San Francisco was empty of the kinds of myths familiar to them in rural America or the Old World.

Vaudeville would fill the spiritual gap. As ritual, it would delve deeply beneath the prejudices of the time, crossing religious, geographical, and moral boundaries. To be sure, vaudeville's myth-making capacity relied upon a certain degree of backstage contrivance, and, of course, there was always the pressure to make the ritual conform to the aesthetic standards of American society. But by and large, myths developed out of the intimate contact between performer and audience. I would suggest to you, my darling, that from this process of trial and error arose patterns of symbolic meaning, eventually forming the spectral myths of a new industrial democracy (in particular, the American Dream). Vaudeville was a means by which the soul-devouring experience of immigration and acclimatization slowly would become objectified and accepted.

But who, my sweet, delivered these myths to the masses? Who would step into the fray and fight tooth and nail for the spiritual health of this brave new world? It would be in the mammoth theaters of Keith, Proctor, Considine, and Pantages, as well as in the smalltime "family circuits," that a new type of holy fool would appear: the vaudevillians. They were a ragtag collection of minstrels, dog trainers, and crossdressers, disparate in their practice but unified in their desire to rekindle the dreams of a downtrodden people.

There was "Think-a-Drink" Hoffman, who would stand on stage with nothing in his hands but a large pitcher, seemingly filled with ordinary drinking water. Asking a member of his audience if they would like a cocktail, he would pour whatever they requested: beer, champagne, red or white wine, martinis (with olives), Bloody Marys, crème de menthe, and, for his grand finale, pousse-café. There was Alfred Latell, a specialist in the impersonation of animals. Latell began his career in 1902 and rapidly gained notoriety for his impersonations of monkeys, billy goats, bears, and dogs. He was a slave to his career, creating an artificial joint for his legs (that enabled him to better move as a dog) and a tube for his mouth (that permitted him to lap up milk like a cat).

Minstrel shows were common at the time. They featured all-white casts of men who would perform song and dance in blackface, interspersed with comedy routines that generally featured a pair of endmen universally known as Bruder Tambo and Bruder Bone. Ventriloquists were also popular. One, Sandra Powell, performed an act in the middle of which her dummy fell apart. Powell would break down crying, revealing to her audience that she knew nothing about ventriloquism and that the dummy's voice had been provided by a man hiding offstage. Female impersonators like Gilbert Sarony, Everett

Stuart (billed as "Stuart, the male Patti") and Bert "Swishy" Savoy always played to packed houses. And, of course, my lamb, there was striptease, which began as acts of "living models" or *tableaux vivants,* in which women, and sometimes men, would strike artistic poses while clad in sheer body stockings. Florence Ziegfeld would later modify these acts for his Follies, in which scantily clad showgirls would remain motionless in their careful poses. Noted among the fleshy ranks of striptease are such goddesses as Millie de Leon, Edna Victoria, Carrie "The Girl with the Million Dollar Legs" Finnell, and, of course, Gypsy Rose Lee.

Oh, my beloved, many thought that vaudeville would never die. But, when the Palace Theatre at Broadway and 47th Street in New York closed in May of 1932, it was widely felt that the heart of vaudeville had finally stopped beating. The movie industry had stepped in to take its place. Nevertheless, the story was far from over. Vaudeville did not pass away. The Holy Fools did not die. Their spirits were simply sucked up like Dorothy in that big black and white whirlwind, flung over the rainbow, and deposited where they were needed most. Who could have guessed that they would touch down later in the century in the lounges of Las Vegas and within the hallowed halls of contemporary art? But, whoa, nelly, let's back up a little, my sweet love muffin. Let's look closely together at the construction of the two roosts upon which the "happy little bluebird," the soul of vaudeville, would alight.

In the early nineteen hundreds, artists, like the

bedazzled immigrants we spoke of earlier, were also facing a world of new technology. The work of Etienne-Jules Marey and Eadweard Muybridge in instantaneous photography (called chronophotography) had a profound effect on artists of the period and would lead to a movement known as Futurism. The Futurists held in common a deep interest in time and motion. In 1911, Carlo Carrà would depict motion in *Funeral of the Anarchist Galli,* and one year later Giocomo Balla would paint the sublime *Dynamism of a Dog on a Leash.* As I'm sure you know, my love, in that same year Marcel Duchamp would paint *Nude Descending a Staircase, No. 2,* one of the most controversial paintings of its time. Duchamp began to challenge the very notion of object-based art and pushed, instead, for an "art of the conceptual." His notion (which permeated the movement known as Dadaism) that no material is out of place as a means of personal expression—that "everything is art"—would come to be lovingly embraced, once the avant-garde, having languished a bit from the late nineteen twenties and into the forties, picked up its stride again and began moving forward at a furious pace. You might, my darling, think of Marcel as Moses, an artistic iconoclast leading his followers for forty years through an art desert, finally finding an oasis, a Promised Land, the America of the nineteen fifties. There, performance art would bloom, and vaudeville would be reborn—just as it would be in another oasis located out in the middle of the desert Mojave: a "land of bilk and honeys" called Las Vegas.

From 1938 until the early nineteen fifties, the

groundwork was laid . . . singers, comedians, strippers, instrumentalists, dancers, and a wide variety of performers were booked to entertain hotel guests in the resorts' small, intimate showrooms, with no charge of admission save the cost of a single drink. There was Pearl Bailey ("Porgy and Bess"), Earnie Baron, South American dance team The Robertos, Sonyar Yarr, Woody Wilson, Nick Stuart and his Orchestra, The Radio Aces, and Paula Drake. But singing and dancing was only part of the extravaganza. Between lounge performances, a drunken priest known as "Father Bilko" might approach you, belching loudly as he tried desperately to get you to contribute to his "home for wayward Vegas youth." There was Grock the Clown (Swiss-born Karl Adrian Wettach), who, having been the highest paid artist at one time in Europe, went broke after buying a circus tent for his variety show during World War II. He ended up in Las Vegas, riding a tiny bicycle and balancing on a large multicolored ball for audiences at Thomas Hull's El Rancho.

The Minsky Brothers, famous for their raunchy performances starring Gypsy Rose Lee, Pigmeat Markham, and Abbott and Costello, landed at the Desert Inn in 1950 with Minsky's Follies, the first topless revue in Sin City. Harold Minsky (the adopted son of Abe, one of the original brothers) later would present shows at the Dunes, the Silver Slipper, the Thunderbird, the Aladdin, and the Fremont. And there was the small-time Amy Swaine, who, in 1967, wandered along the strip with a show called "Swaine's Rats and Cats," in which two rats, dressed like jockeys complete with little riding crops taped to their paws, would race around Amy's legs riding a pair of befuddled felines.

But, my darling, just as those little rodents were whipping their mewing steeds beneath a hot, Nevada sun, back East something else was getting a good stroking: Nam June Paik's back. In the 1967 performance *Sextronique,* Paik's shirtless back served as the "bass" for musician Charlotte Moorman's bow. For this little concert, the two would be arrested, but not before Paik could exclaim to the media, "I wanted to stir up the dull waters of sexless men and women in black suits playing music." You see, my darling, artists of the late nineteen fifties and early sixties had grown weary of the rugged, gestural Abstract Expressionism that had come to epitomize American art. There was a restlessness, a need to see something *done.* A yearning for ritual. Pop art would emerge, along with the multimedia experiments of John Cage and his Black Mountain College collaborators. And, my dear, there was "intermedia" Fluxus, an international movement whose members made jabs at the notion that art was the exclusive property of museums and collectors. Indeed, my love, their work functioned to turn mundane ritual into fine art.

For example, LaMonte Young's 1960 *Piano Piece for David Tudor # 2* consisted simply of this direction: "Open the keyboard cover without making, from the operation, any sound that is audible to you. Try as many times as you like." Through minimal instruction, the event opened itself up to multiple interpretations, as well as accidents. Chance ruled, not logic. Bruce Nauman began to make work in which the presence of an implied audience was represented by the video camera . . . watching as he went about a seemingly endless number of mundane activities. Nauman's film *Slow Angle Walk (Beckett Walk)* of 1968 shows the artist walking stiff-leggedly around his studio, lifting one leg high into the air, then swiveling his body in a half turn before letting the leg land on the floor.

Furthermore, one cannot look even briefly into the past of performance without seeing the Viennese Actionists staring into one's eyes. Otto Meuhl's *Funebre* of 1966 presents a naked body lying on a bed, sprayed with pigment, and manipulated by other naked figures. Another of Meuhl's works, *Scheiss-Kerl (Shit Guy)* of 1969, depicts an act of coprophilia. At the heart of the work lies the notion that through destruction comes rebirth; through death, there awaits new life. In the footsteps of the Actionists followed such artists as Orlan, who, since 1974, has been in the process of resculpting her body through plastic surgery in order to transform herself into a composite of historically idealized female forms.

But, my darling, as I sit here in this run-down little motel room, trying to convince you that I am not crazy, I know that I am on a fool's errand. Listing only a few of my favorites, I have left out much of relevance, but a history lesson isn't the point of this missive. I would like to propose to you something more. These vaudevillians, these lounge performers, these performance artists—you are probably already starting to see that they aren't all that different from one another. Please continue with me for a moment along this train of thought. For if you do, I think you will come to believe what I already know in my heart—that they serve a purpose. A higher purpose. The one, true purpose of God: to humbly serve humanity.

Look how closely they are linked. When Bruce Nauman put on clown make-up in 1987 and stood on one leg for *Clown Torture*, screaming "No, No, No," is he enacting a ritual any different from that of Bruder Tambo in a vaudevillian minstrel show? or Grock the Clown, when he rode his little bicycle pathetically before a group of oil tycoons from Houston? or, for that matter, some early Christian monk who was led around wearing the head of a mule during the Feast of Fools? I don't think so. When Siegfried turns Roy into a white tiger, is his act of transformation all that different from Alfred Latell's, sitting on stage in his cat suit, making the hair on his back stand up with a quick pull of the string wrapped around his groin? or from that of contemporary artist Tamara Fites, dressed as Lambi Kins, a bleating half-animal that puts itself humbly within the grasp of her art audience, for good or for ill?

Are the actions of any of these art-entertainers different from that of the thirteenth-century Jacopone da Todi, running around naked, begging for someone to mount him in order to find Jesus? I think not. And, my dear, when Vanessa Beecroft corrals a herd of New York models into a little room and makes them stand naked before an audience, is the picture you get substantially different from the *tableaux vivants* of early vaudeville or the "Showgirls of Magic" at the San Remo in Las Vegas, where nightly you may see topless women performing perplexing prestidigitation? Well, my love, you got me. One difference I can see is that the showgirls *do* stuff, and you get a free cocktail, to boot!

I hope you see that there is an important history here. A history that I intend to join. Is it mad to have such an aspiration? These men and women, these holy fools, these vaudevillians, are sacrificing their minds and bodies for the purpose of returning ritual to social practice. Regardless of whether any of them admit it, the main thing that they share is an audience. A congregation. Pilgrims who come to each of them in order to find an earthly manifestation of all the questions, all the darkness, and all the light that is swirling around within the collective human soul. Jacopone, Francis, Nauman, Fites, McCarthy, Beecroft, and me, the Rev. Ethan Acres . . . we are servants of the flock, performing rituals to purge the longing and uncertainty from those who come before us, broken and alone.

My darling, did you know that Noah was a performance artist, too? It is written in the Apocryphal Book of Enoch, that after Noah, his wife, children, and all of the animals had been on the ocean for a long time, Noah began to hit the bottle a little hard. God became angry and decided that saving Noah and his kin was a mistake. So He brought upon the Ark a great whirlwind that threatened to sink Noah and all those with him beneath the waves. But, in the face of this calamity, Noah drunkenly laughed at God, tore off his clothes, and, ignoring the lightening and the waves, began to dance and sing at the top of his lungs. What do you think God did? He looked down at that crazy, drunken fool . . . and He laughed. He decided to give Noah another chance.

My love, I'm going to quit writing now. I'm tired of New Mexico. I think I'm going to climb into our truck and drive as fast as I can to Texas, where I know you are waiting for me. I don't know what our future holds . . . I'm not certain myself of my sanity, and I'm afraid that there probably are storms waiting out there where the road kisses the sky. But what say, once I get to Texas, we stand up in the bed of this 1994 Ford F-150, rip off all our clothes and sing at the top of our lungs. Let's fill our future with performance—with ritual, action, and love. I think God will forgive us if we cross the line. In fact, if I work it just right, I think He will laugh.

Benediction

". . . AND THE OMEGA."

MY BROTHERS AND SISTERS, I've been doing a lot of traveling lately, spending much of my time out on the road. I've been searching for God, you see. On these trips, I've used every kind of vehicle known to the modern age: I've puttered along in cars, sped along in trains, sailed in old boats, and soared above in great planes. But I think I've always found God at those journeys' ends, when I step off that plane, bus, or train and into the embrace of one I call friend. I'm sure you all know what I'm talking about: those familiar arms holding you tight and those hot kisses on your cheeks and lips. In that heat, in that overwhelming passion, there is God. I can still remember one particular trip, a car trip to be precise, when I came closest to really understanding the Divine.

The year was 1979. I was nine years old. My mother was a librarian at an elementary school in a town called Valley Head, Alabama. She was also an organist for a small Baptist Church. In fact, it was there where she had met my step-father, the Rev. Albert Satcher. Albert was pretty cool, most of the time. Even when he made me stand up in front of church and read scripture, and even when he made me pass out his pamphlets in Ft. Payne, I still loved him. He could tell great stories, and, well, he met God once when he was a little boy. That was the kicker. When he told the story, his eyes would light up like a Christmas tree, and he would turn all red, little beads of sweat breaking out on his forehead, like those pearls my Granny liked to wear to Red Lobster. But I think the thing that fascinated many of my friends the most was not that Albert once had met God. This was Alabama, my beloved, and you couldn't throw a rock without hitting someone who claimed to have met God. No, it wasn't his divine appointment that got my buddies' blood pumping. It was the fact that Albert, in this pact he had made with the Lord, had lost both his arms in the bargain. That's right, both arms. Burned clean off, right below the elbow!

Usually, I hardly noticed, because Albert always wore his prosthetics. And not the ones with the hooks. No sir, these looked just like hands, with flesh-colored rubber skin that even had fingernails molded right in. Sometimes, he would let me roll the "skin" back so I could look at the cogs and springs that made them open and close. And he could do anything with them. He could eat with them and tie his shoes. He could change the oil in our car, and he used to amaze everyone when he made pancakes, flipping the cakes up into the air just like they did on television. I would fib a little in school, convincing people that he actually possessed superhuman strength because of the arms. My friends would call him "The Six Million Dollar Man," especially when he would pick me up at school wearing his red and white sweatsuit. But like I said, I usually didn't notice the arms, since I never saw him without them. Never, ever. Until one Sunday, that is, when his life, and mine, changed forever.

The Six Million Dollar Man. Well, not quite. You have to understand, Albert was what was known as a "circuit preacher." Money was tight and my mother was pregnant—and, well, most of the congregations in North Alabama didn't have a whole lot of spare change to drop into the collection plate. So, Albert made ends meet by preaching regularly at three or four churches each Sunday. "Running the circuit," if you see what I mean. So each Sabbath, my mother and I would squeeze into our lemon-yellow 1976 Toyota Corolla next to Albert, who would drive like a maniac to some little back-woods church, give them a good dose of rip-roaring Hellfire and Brimstone, shake some hands, kiss some babies, and then herd us back into the little car, only to race to the next church and do the whole thing again. Three or four times each Sunday, not to mention the midweek services that some nights would keep us out until one or two in the morning. It was hard work, but it was the only way Albert could keep us fed and the Toyota running and, well, it was the only way Albert could afford his monthly trips to Birmingham, to get his arms repaired.

See, friends, those arms were pretty worn. He had bought them in 1965, and, as far as I could tell hadn't taken them off once since that very day. Sometimes, the right thumb would just mysteriously fall off, and the pinky on the left was always cocked out at an angle that made Al look like some high-society débutante, whenever he drank coffee. But the Reverend didn't care. He loved them, those arms. And he couldn't afford another pair like them; so, instead, he regularly went to Birmingham to have them resprung, or the thumb rewelded, or the rubber skin patched with glue. And I never complained about those Sundays, just spending the services lying beneath the pews at the back of churches, drawing pictures of Godzilla and the Shogun Warriors on the back of church bulletins. And my mother never asked Albert to just take the foolish-looking arms off, knowing full well that it just wouldn't do any good. No, Albert was set in his ways, and those arms were a part of him. As they say, love is blind—which I guess means that you just can't see it coming, when the object of your affection betrays you.

The "Sunday When Everything Changed" started out just like any other. Me being pulled away from the television screaming, "I want to watch UltraMan!!" Then the manic race to the first church. The high-pitched "hallelluiahs" and "hosannas," followed by rousing handshaking, babykissing, and a mad rush to the next church. This happened twice, but, alas, my lambs, somewhere along the way, we fell behind. And, to our dismay, we left one church at the very time when our service at the next was scheduled to begin. Albert hadn't even had time to take off his robe, and as we furiously sped up Highway 11, my mother had to hold the billowing black fabric down, so the Reverend could see to drive.

I never knew that our Toyota could go so fast. I think that was the first time I ever put on a seatbelt, so scared was I at the sight of all the fields and farms flashing by, blurring into some sickly yellow and green goo outside the windows of the little car. Albert ground the gears, and I could hear his foot repeatedly slamming into the floor of the Corolla, as if pumping the pedal would in some way make the gas flow just a little faster.

Up into Sand Mountain we sped, and before long we had passed into the town called Ider, and, to my relief, as I bounced to and fro in the backseat, I could see our destination, Sand Mountain Baptist Church, speeding toward us like a locomotive. With a yell of victory, and my mother clapping her hands, Albert spun the little car into the parking lot, dust and stone flying up into the bright blue afternoon sky. Creaking on its springs, the little car came to a stop. My mother reached over and turned off the ignition, and Albert said, "Let's hustle!"

But, my Brothers and Sisters, as Albert tried to remove his arms from the steering wheel, there was a loud crack. A snap, really. Like the sound a twig makes when you step on it in the middle of the winter. And, to his dismay, and our horror, Albert realized that he couldn't make the arms let go of the steering wheel.

At first, the Reverend just laughed. He gently began twisting the arms back and forth, hoping that through the use of a little leverage, the fingers would release. This went on to no avail. Then Albert tried quick little jerks, but again, the arms wouldn't let go. It didn't take long before Albert was violently banging back and forth, desperately trying to unlock the fingers from the steering wheel. But the arms held firm, clenching the wheel like a Mississippi snapping turtle. He shook and shook and shook, the Toyota rocking back and forth, and then, for the first time in my life, I heard a man of God, *my* man of God, begin to curse.

"DAMN YOU, GOD! DAMN YOU! How dare you do this to me. I've done all that you asked, you sonofabitch! I took in this woman and her son, I've done your work, and I have given you EVERYTHING I HAVE! Hell, I even gave you my arms. But now, how do you repay me? You, oh WONDERFUL God, leave me here, stuck in this Japanese piece of crap, on the side of the road, with no help at all! DAMN YOU!!!!

"And what, God, do you think that those people in there, waiting for me, will say when they come out and see this mess I'm in? Do you think they'll be all helpful and kind, hmmm? All Christian? HELL, NO!!! They'll laugh. They'll point. They'll say 'Look at the poor cripple stuck in his pathetic car.' That's what they'll say, DAMN YOU!"

Soon, Albert's curses just blended together into some unrecognizable language of the profane, as he continued to jerk back and forth against the steering wheel. I don't know how long this lasted, but there finally came a point when I realized that he had stopped, his head resting against the wheel.

My friends, it was one of those moments when it seems like the world slows down just a little. I remember that the windows in the car had fogged over, and droplets of water were slowly making their way down the glass, leaving little snail trails behind them. I remember my mother crying, her hands covering her face, her bright red fingernails contrasting sharply against her pale skin. I remember the smell of sweat mixed with the Chanel No. 5 that Albert always bought my mother on her birthday. And I remember the sound of an organ being played in the church, spilling from windows opened in defiance to the hot summer afternoon. For an eternity, I fiddled with a loose thread sticking out of the cuff of my pants. But, as all moments pass, so did this one, and Albert finally raised his head. As best he could, he turned back, staring into my eyes, and began to speak.

"Son, do you have that pocketknife I gave you for Christmas?"

"Yes sir, I do," I stammered, curious, and a little bit frightened at the prospect of a knife being brought into all of this.

"Well, son, I need you to do something for me." I had never heard Albert's voice sound so old before. "I want you to take out that knife, and cut a little hole in the back of my robe. Then I want you to reach in, and find the straps that hold these arms on, and son, I want you to cut them. Cut the straps loose. Get me out of this car."

So, my friends, I reached into the pocket of my pants and pulled out the little knife that had been in my Christmas stocking only a few months before. I loved that knife. It had Luke Skywalker on it. It was still new and shiny, and I fumbled with it, trying to get it open. My hands were too sweaty, so instead I put the blade in my teeth and pulled the knife open. I could taste the oil on my tongue . . . bitter.

Reaching forward, I cut a small hole in Albert's robe, and gingerly reached in. His back was clammy, drenched in sweat, but I said nothing. I searched carefully, mindful of how easily the blade of my knife had cut through the robe's fabric, until finally I found the straps. Slowly, I pushed the blade between the straps and Albert's shoulder. I then turned the blade and pulled, feeling a satisfying give as the strap was cut and the tension broke.

I sat back against my seat as Albert used his hip to pop open the driver's door, and then I watched as my stepfather stepped out into the sunlight, leaving those two arms hanging there, all by themselves on the steering wheel of the car. It now seems that I stared at those arms for a long time, marveling at the way they glowed in the bright light, their little silver buckles on the straps glinting like fireflies. But that couldn't have been the case, for my mother's Lee Press-On claws dug into my arm as she pulled me harshly out into the parking lot, pushing me into a run as we chased Albert into the church.

She and I stood panting at the back and watched as the Reverend slowly walked to the front of the chapel. His head was down, and his back was bent as if all the weight of the world was pressing down upon him. The sanctuary had grown quiet, even the organist had quit playing. When he climbed to the pulpit, he turned, raised his head, and looked out at the congregation. I could see tears in his eyes, and I could hear my mother's breathing stop.

Then, Albert raised his empty sleeves, fleshy nubs peeking

out of the dark folds, and he began to preach.

And, my friends, I'm here to tell you that on that day Albert preached the greatest sermon of his life. Fire burned in his eyes and leapt from his tongue. His body rocked back and forth like a ship braving the mightiest of storms. He danced and yelled, and was Baptized in the Spirit. By the end of the sermon, every person in the church had come forward to receive God, and then stayed to put their arms around this Man of God. Albert had come to the end of a journey, and what did he find waiting for him there? The open arms of people who loved him, holding him tight, planting hot kisses on his cheeks and lips, and telling him, "We love you." Albert was whole again. He was THE MAN. He was home. And all he had to do was leave pride behind—hanging on the steering wheel of a 1976 Toyota Corolla.

That day I decided to be a preacher, but, unknowingly, I became an artist. For there, in that little church, I caught my first fleeting glimpse of the eternal beauty which men greater than I have named the human soul. On that day, I felt the presence of God. It would not be the last time, either.

But this is a story for another day.

Acknowledgments

TOUP DREAMS was originally published in *Art issues* #59 (September/October 1999). THE STRAIGHT OR CROOKED WAY was originally published in *Art issues* #56 (January/February 1999). VIRTUAL HEAVEN was originally published in *Art issues* #62 (March/April 2000). EXERCISING DEMONS was originally published in *Art issues* #65 (November/December 2000). DEAR JERRY was originally published as A LETTER OF CONSANGUINITY in *Art issues* #66 (January/February 2001). PERFORMANCE ANXIETY was originally published in *Art issues* #68 (Summer 2001).

About the Author

After receiving a Bachelor's Degree from the University of Texas in Austin, a young man named Ethan Acres, like the prophets of old, wandered into the desert to find God. He found Him in the burning neon of Las Vegas, Nevada. Ordained by World Christianship Ministries in 1995, he was awarded an Honorary Doctorate of Divinity from World Christianship in 1996, the same year he graduated with an M.F.A. from the University of Nevada, Las Vegas. An artist, as well as a man of God, the Reverend has shown his work and presided over weddings, funerals, baptisms, and a number of esoteric rituals across the globe. He is also the caretaker of Nevada's only chapel on wheels, The Highway Chapel, a converted 1965 Shasta Camper Trailer. In the secular world, he is represented by Patricia Faure Gallery in Los Angeles, California.

Currently, the Right Reverend lives out on the road with his beautiful wife Lisa, their son Cyrus, and their trusty dog Achilles. He fights to defeat the Devil in all his evil forms and strives to put the "fun" back into Fundamentalism.

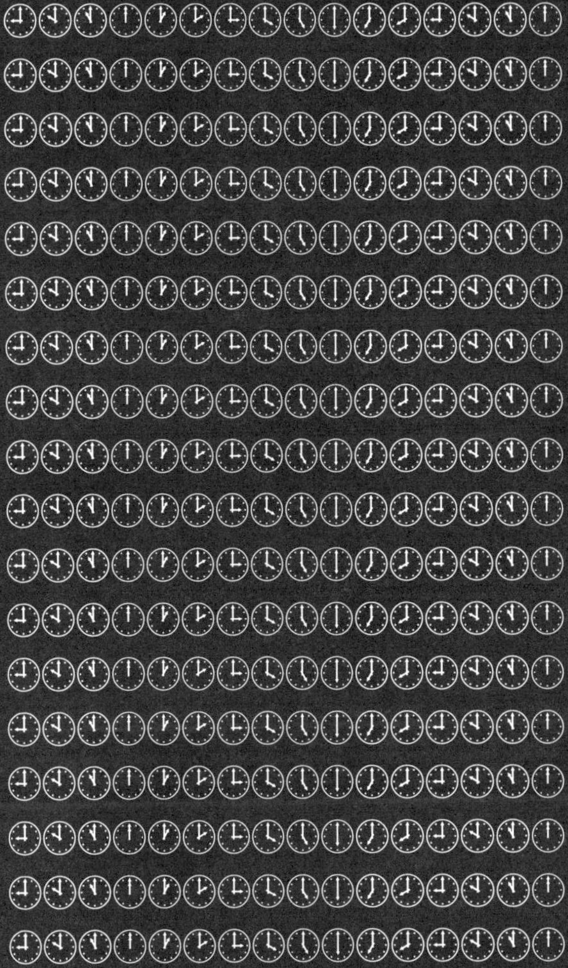

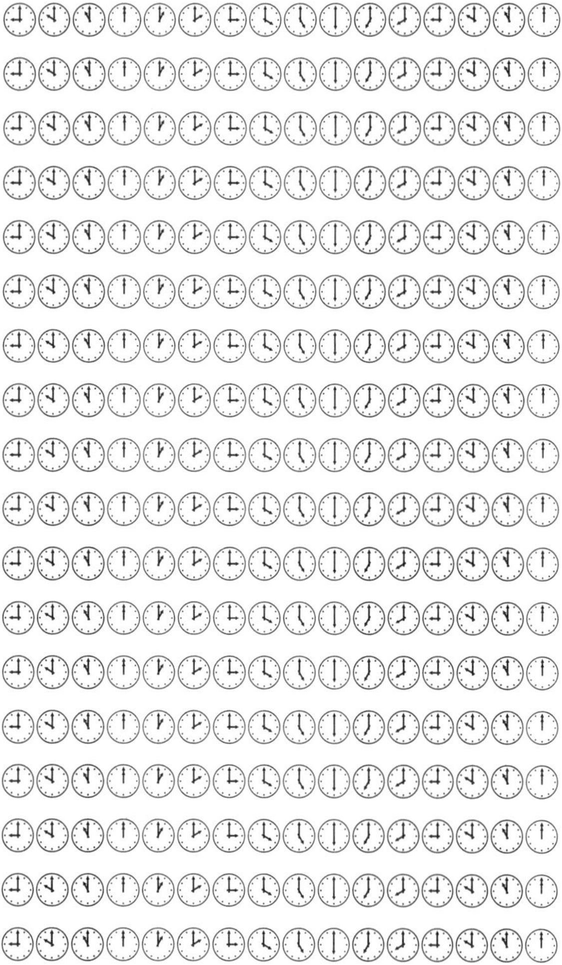

COLOR PLATES, WITH

Cookin' for the Rev., by Rev. Mrs. Acres

Friends, at the end of the day, do your partner's eyes look lifeless and dull? Is all the spring sprung right out of his step? Bake him a batch of scrumdidilicious treats and put him back on his game with my . . .

Snickerdoodles

FIRST, YOU NEED:
1-1/2 cups sugar
1/2 cup butter, softened
1/2 cup shortening
2 eggs
1 tsp. vanilla
3 cups self-rising flour
3 tbs. sugar
1 tbs. cinnamon

THEN:
1. Preheat oven to 400°.
2. Cream sugar, butter, and shortening.
3. Beat in eggs and vanilla until light and fluffy.
4. Stir in flour just until blended.
5. Combine the sugar and cinnamon in a small bowl.
6. Shape dough into 1-inch balls and roll in sugar-cinnamon mixture.
7. Place on baking sheet 2-inches apart and bake for 6–7 minutes or until set around the edges. Cool.

Yields 6 dozen cookies.

✝

Rev. Ethan Acres as witness to a healing session with Ernest Angley, 1979

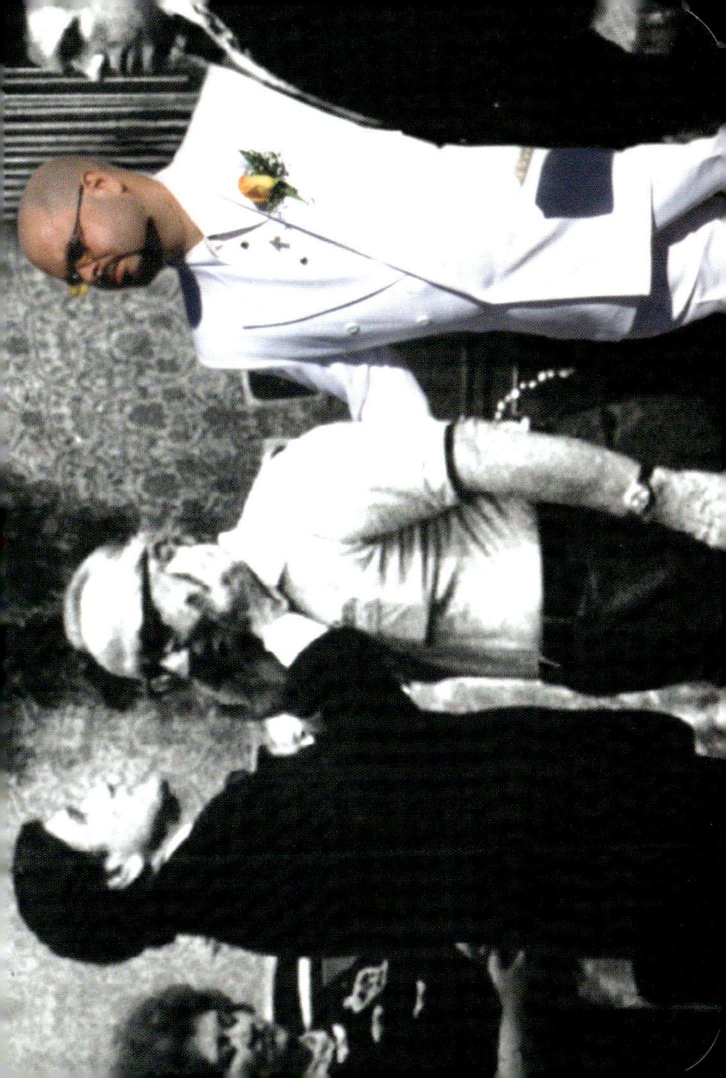

Boy, does the Reverend love Dump Cake! He once told me that it could "make the lame walk and the blind see." Well, I don't know about that, but I do know that it sure can make a southern boy run . . . for the dinner table, that is!

Dump Cake

FIRST, YOU NEED:

1 large can crushed pineapple with juice
1 can pie filling (cherry or apple)
1 box yellow cake mix (sprinkle over pie filling)
1 cup chopped nuts (optional)
2 sticks Oleo, cut in pats

THEN:

1. Preheat oven to 350°.
2. Layer the ingredients in the order that they appear above.
3. Bake 1 hour, or until done.

†

Rev. Ethan Acres at the Bellagio Resort & Casino, 1998

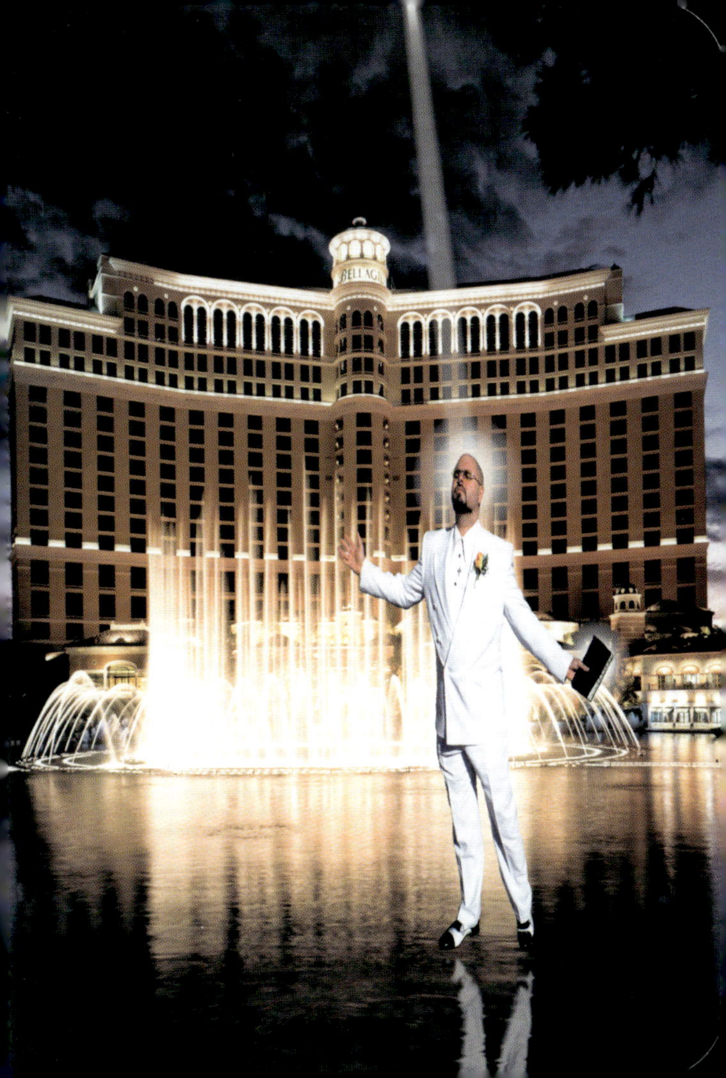

More than anything else, the Reverend loves to have snacks around the house. But I like to slip in something wholesome and good for him. You can too with my scrumptious . . .

Cookies from the Garden of Eatin'

FIRST, YOU NEED:

3 cups old-fashioned oats
1 cup all-purpose flour
1 tsp. ground cinnamon
1/2 tsp. baking soda
1/4 tsp. salt
1/2 cup (1 stick) unsalted butter, at room temperature
1/4 cup solid vegetable shortening
3/4 packed light-brown sugar
1/2 cup granulated sugar
1 egg
1/4 cup water
1 tsp. vanilla
1 cup milk-chocolate chips
3/4 cup chopped dried apricots (4 to 5 ounces)
1/2 cup golden raisins
1/2 cup dried cherries

THEN:

1. Preheat oven to 350°.
2. Mix oats, flour, cinnamon, baking soda, and salt in a bowl.
3. On medium-high speed (or you can do this by hand, it just takes longer), beat butter and shortening in a large bowl until creamy. Beat in the brown and granulated sugars until fluffy. Beat in the egg and water. Beat in the vanilla.
4. On low speed, beat in oat mixture. Fold in chips, apricots, raisins, and cherries. Drop by heaping tablespoonfuls, about 2-inches apart, onto ungreased cookie sheet.
5. Bake in oven 10 to 12 minutes, until browned. Cool slightly on pan. Transfer to rack to cool.

Rev. Ethan Acres in Rapture at the Getty Museum, 1999

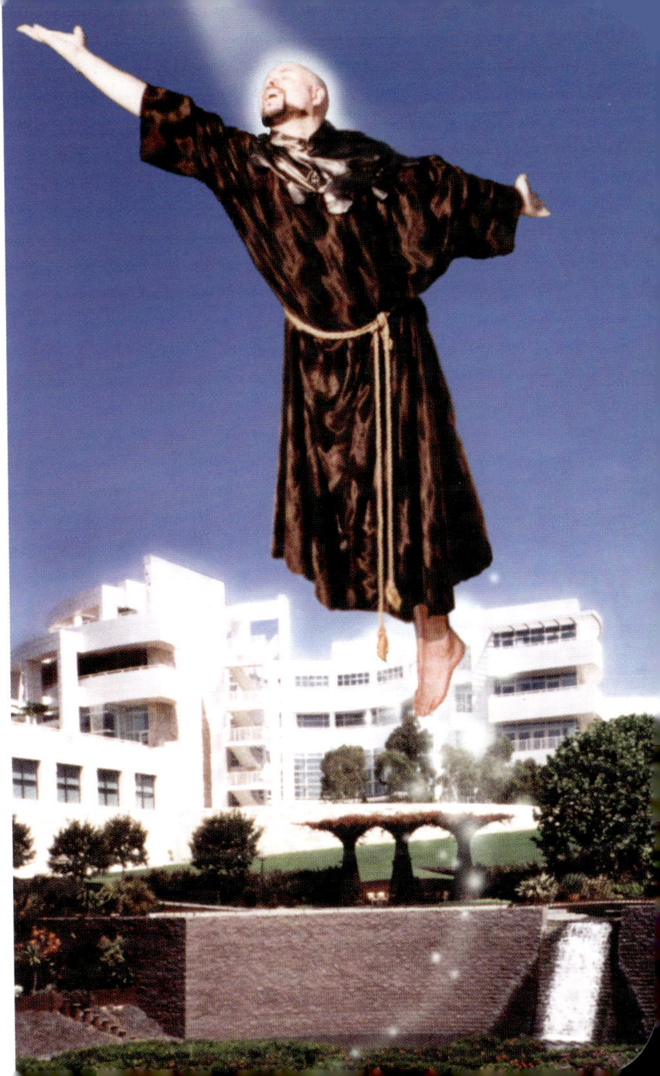

My man sure works up an appetite after a long day of preaching. There is one thing that is guaranteed to satisfy his hunger, a mouth-watering brisket. And when you see how easy it is to make, you'll want to cook one up for yourself.

Texas-style Brisket

FIRST, YOU NEED TO ROUND UP:

1 beef brisket (go ahead and get a big one, it makes for a great sandwich)
1 bottle of liquid smoke
1 bottle of your favorite BBQ sauce
Lawry's Seasoned Salt or a good beef seasoning
Garlic salt
Meat tenderizer
Celery salt
Pepper

THEN:

1. Preheat oven to 250°.
2. Line roasting pan with heavy duty aluminum foil, leaving enough to completely cover brisket.
3. Pour entire bottle of liquid smoke over brisket. Generously sprinkle on meat tenderizer and seasoned salt. Then sprinkle on garlic, celery salts, and pepper.
4. Completely cover brisket with tinfoil and place in oven.
5. Bake for 5 hours. Remove brisket and gently open foil. Pour entire bottle of BBQ sauce over brisket. Cover tightly and return to oven for 1 more hour.
6. Slice and serve.

Rev. Ethan Acres performing an exorcism at the Santa Monica Museum of Art, Good Friday, March 13, 2001

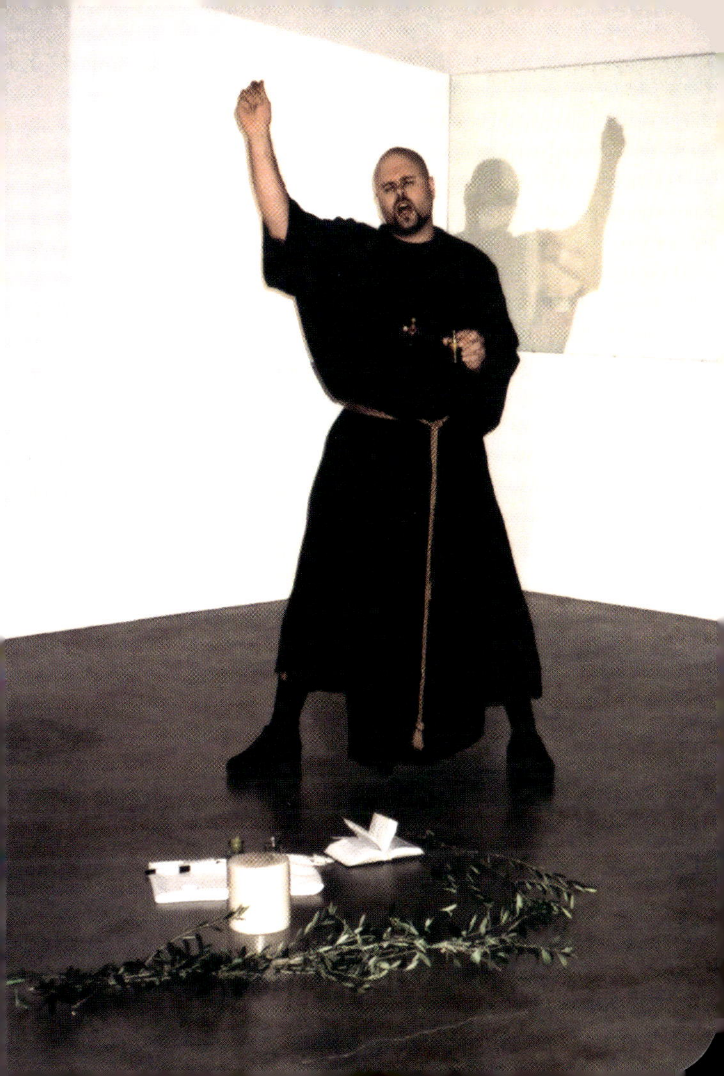

Sometimes, my sweetie gets the foolish notion in his head that he needs to lose weight. But one bite of shrimp creole always sets his mind at ease . . . especially if it's as hot as hell!

Shrimp Creole

FIRST, SAUTÉ UNTIL TENDER, BUT NOT BROWNED:
1/4 cup butter
2 medium onions, diced
1 cup celery, diced
1 clove garlic, minced
1/2 lb. fresh mushrooms, sliced

NEXT, BLEND IN:
2 tbsp. flour
1/2 tsp. salt (optional)
1/8 tsp. pepper
1/4 tsp. paprika
1/2 tsp. chili powder

THEN, ADD:
4 drops Tabasco sauce (add some more, and start exercising your own demons!)
2 fresh tomatoes, diced
1 (14 oz.) can tomato sauce

FINALLY, YOU'RE READY:
1. Cover and simmer for 10 minutes.
2. Add 1 pound cleaned shrimp and cook just until the shrimp turn pink.
3. Mix in 1 sliced green pepper and simmer 3 minutes.
4. Add 1 tsp. sugar (optional).
5. Serve over steamed rice.

Rev. Ethan Acres finding enlightenment while on a Stairmaster, 2000

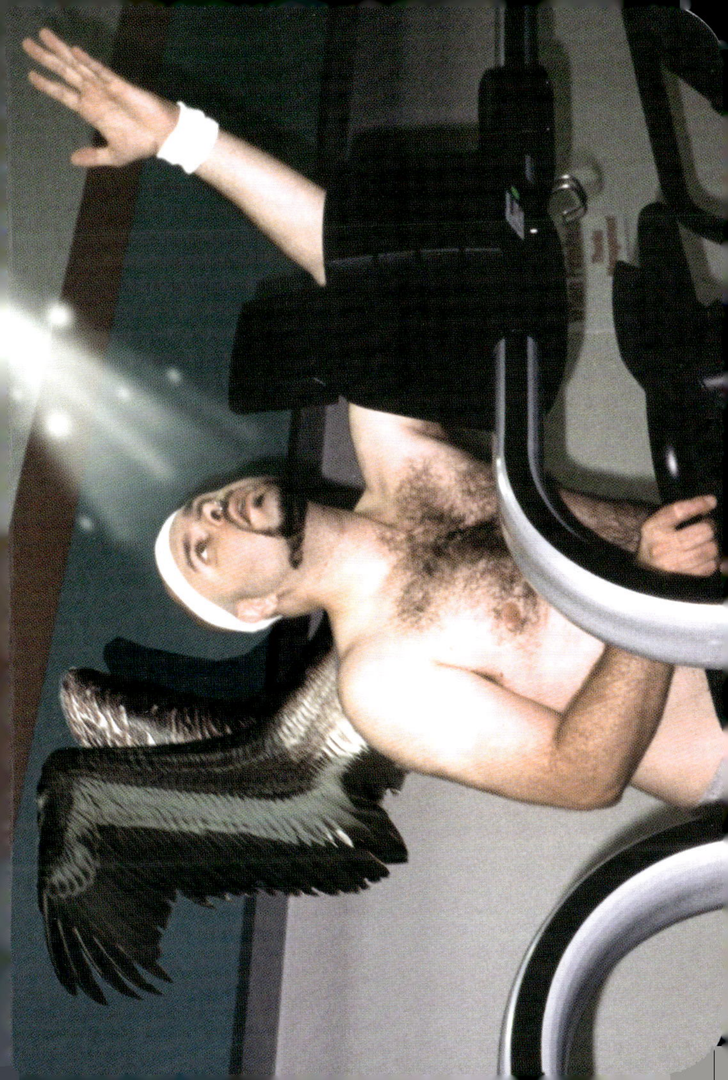

For those long afternoons in the park, when my fella just needs something to tide him over until supper, no appetizer brings a smile to his face like my . . .

Cool Cucumber Sandwiches

FIRST, YOU NEED:

Large loaf of bread
1 (8oz) block cream cheese, softened to room temperature
2 tbsp. grated onion
1 large cucumber peeled, seeded, and grated
1–2 tbsp. mayonaise
Salt and pepper to taste

THEN:

1. Cream the cream cheese. Add mayonaise. Beat.
2. Add remaining ingredients. Stir well.
3. Cool for 10 minutes before making sandwiches.
Spread evenly between two pieces of sliced bread and cut into small, bite-sized squares. Enjoy!

Rev. Ethan Acres as the Teletubbie Tinky Winky, 2000

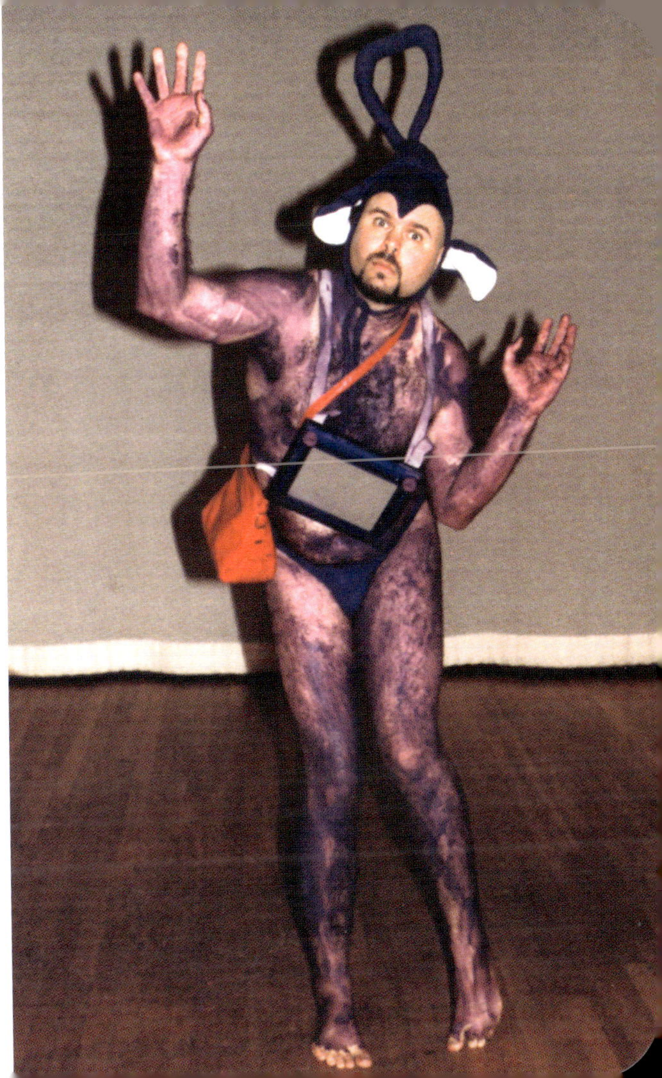

When the bats start flying loose in my big guy's belfry, I find the only thing that will chase those nasty buggers away are my little . . .

Fruit Cake Cookies

FIRST, PLACE TO ONE SIDE:

1/2 lb. green candied cherries
1/2 lb. red candied cherries

NEXT, COMBINE:

1 lb. mixed fruit (dried)
1/2 lb. white raisins
1 lb. chopped pecans
1/2 cup flour

THEN, TO MAKE THE BATTER, MIX TOGETHER:

1/2 cup brown sugar
1/3 cup real butter
2 eggs
1-1/2 cups flour
1/3 cup cooking sherry
2 tsp. soda
1-1/2 tsp. milk
1 tsp. cinnamon
2 tsp. each: cloves, nutmeg, and allspice

FINALLY, YOU'RE READY:

1. Stir the dried fruit mix into the batter.
2. Drop the mixture by teaspoonful onto a greased cookie sheet (or spray it with Pam).
3. Top each cookie with 1/2 green or red candied cherry.
4. Bake at 300° for 30 minutes. Cool and store in an airtight container.

Rev. Ethan Acres as Jacopone da Todi, 2001

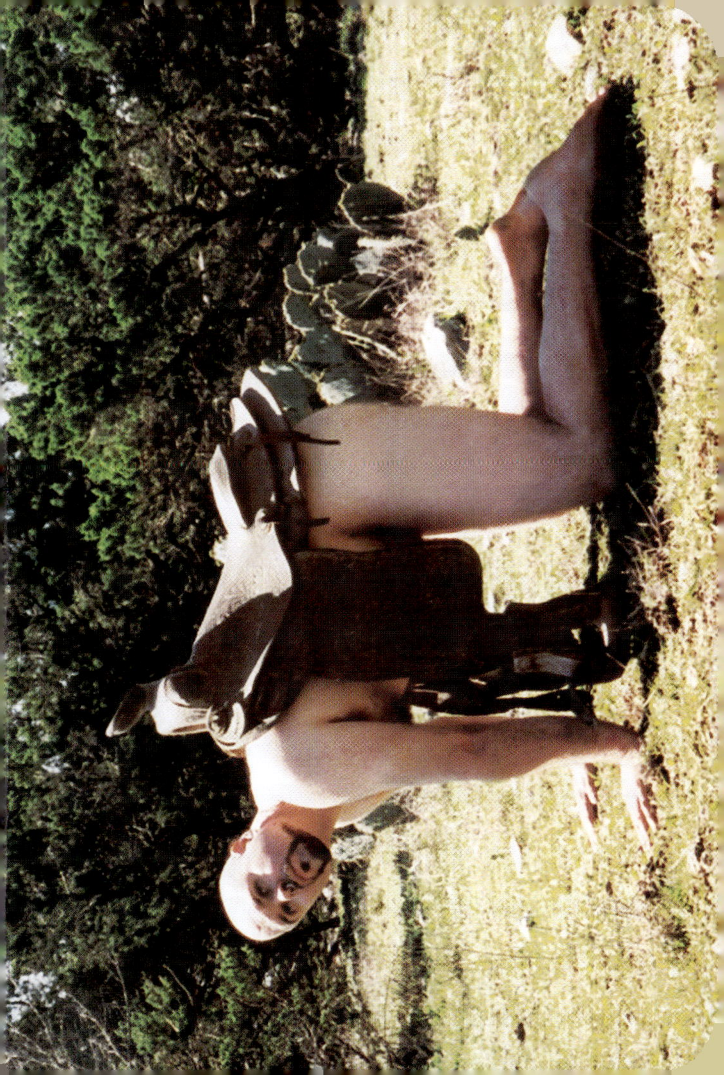

This editon has been designed by Tracey Shiffman and printed by Sinclair Printing Co.
It is printed on Cougar Opaque Vellum 80lb text and McCoy Matte 100lb text and wrapped in Skivertex Pellaq and Carnival Vellum. Sermons are set in FontFont Celeste with heads in Emigre Sabbeth Black. Recipes are set in Emigre Brothers with heads in OptiFont French Script.